The Way
I see it

Nicole Dryburgh

The Way
I see it

Hodder
Children's
Books

A division of Hachette Children's Books

To Mum xxx

There are rules to reading this book.

Do not give me pity – I don't need it.
Do not feel sorry for me – because I'm not sorry.
Do not give me sympathy – I don't want it.
Do not think poor girl – because I'm not.
Do not cry while reading this book – you'll make
the pages wet.
Stick to these rules and we will get along great!

Love Nicole xxx

Contents

Introduction

In the early part of 2000 Nicole Dryburgh was looking forward to her eleventh birthday. Sporty and outgoing, she was always on the go. Seven years later, Nicole is blind, disabled and confined mainly to a wheelchair. She depends on her mother to meet most of her everyday needs.

But Nicole's story – though traumatic – is not a tragedy. She now lives a very different, but full life, surrounded by family and friends, some of whom have contributed their thoughts to this book.

What happened to change Nicole's life so dramatically?

And how did she and those around her cope with those changes?

In early 2000 Nicole was diagnosed with a rare malignant tumour on her spine. An operation at King's College Hospital, London, that August, removed part of it, and she underwent radiotherapy until the end of the year. The doctors were pleased with her progress, until April 2002 when Nicole suffered more serious symptoms, triggering further investigations. An exploratory operation was cancelled when she caught chickenpox, but once she had recovered from that, her symptoms mysteriously disappeared. Not so the underlying problem, though. Nicole became desperately ill that December and was hospitalised, and for the following four months her life hung in the balance.

But against all odds, Nicole came home.

Nicole's story is a remarkable one. Physically she remains weakened by the trauma of her illness and aware that she will never be fully well again. But her personality and character remain undamaged. Supported throughout by her wonderful mother, family and friends, Nicole is as busy as she ever was. Whether she is studying, fundraising, horse-riding, playing with her mischievous dogs or socialising with friends, Nicole is wholehearted and positive – and a role model for all.

Nicole's Story

Me

I was born on 9th February 1989 in Stobhill Hospital, Glasgow, Scotland. I've never liked my surname because no one can say it properly. Dryburgh is pronounced like Edinburgh.

I've never been normal!

I was born with a heart murmur – an irregular heartbeat – but it fixed itself within six months.

Then, when I was about six months old, Nanny said to Mum, 'Can you see that turn in her eye?' My left eye was turned in, so I was cross-eyed! But that corrected itself too.

I didn't have any hair until I was eighteen months old, but I could walk by the time I was nine months. In fact when I was nine months old I climbed out of my cot, walked downstairs and knocked on the living-room door. Mum opened the door and looked down to find little, bald, toothless, cross-eyed me looking up at her. As soon as she put me back in my cot I climbed right back out, so she had to put boards on the sides so that there was nothing for me to grab hold of.

I'm told I was a moany, grizzly, clingy baby, always crying for Mum and demanding to be carried. I'm sure I wasn't that bad. When I was seven, Mum and Dad split up, and I moved with Mum and my brother, Lee, to Kent in England. It took me only six months to lose my Scottish accent. Now we live in a bungalow by the sea in Whitstable. And we have two dogs, Molly and Daizy, who love to walk along the beach.

My mum, Jackie

My mum and I are very close. When I became ill, she gave up her job as a dental nurse to look after me. She's very laid back and tends not to let things bother her, unless Lee or I aren't well. We have similar tastes and the same sense of humour. She's the only person who knows the real me.

My brother, Lee

Lee makes me laugh a lot. We only argue over silly things – the last packet of crisps or something really unimportant like that. He looks out for me and is a brilliant protective big brother. All the girls love Lee. He's a bit of a charmer and a genuinely nice bloke.

My dogs

As far as I am concerned, Molly and Daizy are as human as dogs can be. Molly was my best present ever. She arrived when I first became ill, and like everybody else, she adapted to my illness. She now puts her toys in my hand for me to throw, and when I hear her tapping on the patio doors I crawl to the door to let her in from the garden. Molly has such a pretty face – brown and white with a brown freckle at the side of her mouth that has black whiskers coming out of it. The rest of her mouth is white with white whiskers. I love that brown freckle.

It took a bit of persuasion but in June 2004 Mum finally agreed to a new dog, because Molly's sister had puppies. We called her Daizy because her black and white markings are similar to those of a cow! She learnt quickly because she copied Molly, who was a bit grumpy at first, but within a week they were sharing toys and eating from the same bowl. Although they are very different they miss each other when they are apart.

Both dogs love our company. When I am in bed Daizy sits on my pillow like a hat, or wraps herself round my neck like a scarf. Molly is almost always on my lap, or up my jumper or under my duvet if I am in bed. Her little nose pops out to have a sniff if I'm eating, and she eats up any stray crumbs.

Even more about me!

My favourite colour is pink.
Everything I have is pink.
I am a girlie girl.

I'm told that I'm quite High Maintenance!
But I am a very positive person and always laughing.
And I don't let my disabilities get me down.

I joined St Nicholas' School in Canterbury in the Autumn
Term of 2004. I had one-to-one tuition in art, music,
cooking and English because I couldn't concentrate with
lots of noise around me. I also had physiotherapy there.
Everybody at St Nicholas' School has learning and
physical disabilities, and many use wheelchairs.

I was at the school for two years, and also had lessons
at home in IT and English.

In September 2006 I started at Canterbury
College doing an English GCSE course. I had a support
teacher who came to the lessons with me and wrote
down notes, which she later emailed to me at home to
read through.

Obviously, I used to go to a different school, five days
a week, like any other person. And I hold my hands up –
I wasn't an angel. Once, when I was in primary school in

Scotland – I think I was about six years old – my class was having a plant-growing competition. My plant was winning until my friend's plant overtook mine, so I dug my fingernails into the leaves of hers and it died. The school rang Mum to tell her and I was disqualified – served me right. I remember making quite a few trips to the head teacher's room over the years . . . sometimes it wasn't actually my fault!

I always knew that I wanted to go to Barton Court Grammar School. I'm not sure why, but I did, so I sat the Kent Test and did quite well which meant I was able to go to Barton Court where I met The Girls – my four best friends who have helped me through a lot. I appreciate them for sticking by me over the years because I know it has been difficult. We do different things together these days, but we have so many shared memories and we still make each other laugh.

The Girls

Nicola, Rachel, Charlotte and Kerry visit every week. I don't know what I would do without The Girls. We never argue because we know what we mean to each other and I know they will stick by me. We text each other all the time.

Nicola (Nic) has lovely eyes, thick hair and a beautiful smile. She's the quiet one. She's really caring and a good listener.

Three ways to describe Nic: friendly, cute and kind.

Rachel (Rach) is slim, with long dark hair and greeny-blue eyes. She was my shopping buddy.

Three ways to describe Rach: funny, mad and sweet.

Charlotte (Char) has beautiful big blue eyes and blonde hair. She has got to be the maddest of the lot of us.

Three ways to describe Char: generous, funny and beautiful.

Kerry (Kez) is slim with blue eyes and blonde hair and she is very loud. She always makes me laugh with her 'Kerryisms'.

Three ways to describe Kez: loud, lovely and loyal.

A Pain in the Neck!

2000

February – Scotland, on holiday

I was at the swimming pool and decided to go down the flume one last time, and as I did, I bumped my right arm. Immediately I felt a sharp shooting pain which continued, on and off, for the rest of the holiday.

By the time we came home, the pain was waking me up in the night, and reaching further and further down my arm, so Mum took me to the doctor. I was told to take painkillers, and to come back in a couple of weeks if things didn't improve. They didn't.

Most nights I woke crying with the pain.

Mum's friend – a hypnotherapist – came to see me. It didn't really work and I felt a bit stupid. So she made a tape for me to listen to when I woke up in the night. She talked calmly and quietly about going away in a car made of purple fluffy clouds. But it didn't work and the pain became worse. I would take painkillers and an hour later I would ask for more, but it was too soon. I was only eleven, so I couldn't take very strong tablets.

Eventually my GP referred me to a paediatrician, another doctor who specialises in illnesses in children. He did all the normal tests and then, because I explained that I used to do twelve hours of gymnastics every week, he asked me to show him some stretches. So there I was, in the middle of his tiny room, demonstrating my gymnastic skills. I got the impression he thought that if my arm really hurt, I shouldn't be able to stretch like that. He asked if anything was bothering me at school, and he asked Mum if everything was OK at home. I was upset and annoyed about that; it felt as if people didn't believe me and had decided that I was 'attention seeking'.

I thought what was the point in telling anyone.

After a couple more doctors' appointments I was referred to Jenny Seggie, a physiotherapist at a local children's clinic. She too asked me to demonstrate some exercises and it was when I did a certain stretch, and told her that it hurt, that she decided that the problem was not with my arm but my neck.

She suggested that the pain might be as a result of whiplash, and sent me for an MRI scan – the first of many. It was a very strange experience. The scanner was the size of a small bedroom and because anything metal makes the scan images blurry, I couldn't wear my jeans or a glittery picture on my T-shirt. So I had to borrow hospital pyjamas, which aren't very cool at all. Mum stayed in the room with me, and the radiographers operated the scanner from another room separated from us by a glass window.

Being in a scanner is a bit like being in a tunnel – so I felt quite claustrophobic. I lay on a narrow stretcher-type bed which was fed into the scanner with my face fifteen centimetres from the top. My head was strapped down and I had to lie completely still so that the images they took would be absolutely clear. The bed was moved now and again to scan different parts of my spine. The machine was noisy – like walking past a digger in the street – and I felt quite cold. Mum and I were given earplugs, but they didn't really help. I was very glad to get out of there.

I then went for a series of blood tests in London. What upset me more than anything was that I had to miss my last day at primary school. It was traditional in our school for everyone to sign everybody else's shirts on our final day. All my friends signed my shirt a day earlier so I didn't miss out, but it wasn't the same. My friends kept asking me why I wouldn't be at school the next day, and I remember not knowing what to say, because I didn't really know myself.

My auntie, Lesley, who was on holiday from Scotland at the time, came to the hospital with me, Mum and

Lee. The doctors told us that I might have a condition called neurofibromatosis which could have something to do with the birthmarks I have on my face and leg – they're very faint. (In our family, we all have this kind of birthmark – they are called café au lait, French for milky coffee, which describes their colour exactly.) I had to have a blood test – my first experience with a needle. I remember they used an adult-size needle, when it should have been a child's one. I had to be bribed with a McDonalds to have it done. Mum, Lee and Lesley had to have blood tests too, which I felt guilty about.

The doctors mentioned 'a growth' but that meant nothing to me. I told my friends at school that's what I had and was really annoyed when I heard a boy in my class saying, 'Nicole has a tumour.'

'It's not a tumour, it's a growth!' I shouted.

But I will never forget my teacher's face. She had such a look of pity. I suddenly realised that what the boy had said was true, and that it must be a bad thing.

August – the treatment

The first operation on the top of my spine took place on 7th August 2000. The night before the operation I met the consultant neurosurgeon, Chris Chandler, and as soon as I met him, I liked him. He looked a bit like Willy Wonka from the film, *Charlie and the Chocolate Factory* – the version starring Gene Wilder – with his curly hair, and he had an American accent.

All the children on the ward loved him. He let us pick the hat he would be wearing during our operations – mine was a Union Jack design. That kind of thing kept me going, and stopped me thinking too much about the operation. I wasn't even very nervous, more excited – but at that stage we still didn't understand how serious the situation was.

On the morning of the operation, instead of being worried, I remember being embarrassed because the hospital gown didn't shut properly at the back. I felt very self-conscious as I was wheeled from Lion Ward to the operating theatre in the main part of the hospital. It only started getting a bit scary when we went through some doors to get to the theatre room, which smelt different – clean and sterile. Mum had to put a hairnet on her head and plastic coverings over her shoes and wear a gown. When I went into the room where the operation was going to happen, I looked around and there were lots of machines and a tray with shiny silver scalpels, scissors and lots of other surgical instruments laid out neatly on a green cloth. The room was brightly lit, all white and clean.

The anaesthetist came and stuck sticky pads on my chest to monitor my heart rate. Then a gas mask was placed over my mouth and nose and I was told to count to ten. I don't know what number I reached but it certainly wasn't ten. The gas mask smelt of strawberry to begin with, and then it turned into normal-smelling anaesthetic.

Mum told me later that's when she cried, because she knew, next door, that there was a chocolate-smelling anaesthetic that I would have preferred.

It felt as if I had just dozed off for a couple of minutes. But when I woke, I had been unconscious for five hours – two hours longer than planned. I was groggy and confused. A nurse kept shouting 'Nicole!' in my ear to wake me up. I just wanted to tell her to shut up so that I could sleep but she wouldn't go away. I was sore, and gradually realised that a drip had been put in my hands and my arm.

The next day Chris Chandler told Mum and me that I had a rare type of cancer called a Peripheral Nerve Sheath Tumour. The biopsy revealed it was malignant. He explained that he had been unable to remove the entire tumour because it was so close to my spinal cord. The tumour was pushing on the nerves that went down my right arm. That was why my arm had hurt so much. I still don't think I really understood that the word 'tumour' meant that I had cancer. I was only eleven – I knew nothing about cancer.

I had radiotherapy at the Royal Marsden Hospital in Surrey to kill the rest of the tumour. We had to travel there from Whitstable every day for eight weeks. It was very tiring. To ensure that the radiotherapy rays were going to the same spot every time and weren't killing off the healthy cells, the technicians made a mask of my face. For every treatment the mask would be screwed on to the radiotherapy table, so that I was always lying in exactly the same position.

To make the mask, a mould was made of my head. First, a bandage was pulled over my face and covered in a rubbery solution called alginate. It took about five minutes to set and I didn't like it because I couldn't breathe properly and it all got stuck in my hair. A couple of weeks later I went back to have a mould of the back of my head done – the same procedure but less uncomfortable or scary.

Every day after my radiotherapy treatment, I stuck a sticker on a special chart I'd been given. On the first day, I stuck stickers of Cavalier King Charles spaniels on it because Molly – who was a puppy at the time – is half spaniel and half Jack Russell and there was one sticker that looked just like her. I love stickers and went overboard with them! Other children's charts had one sticker for each day but I would use as many as I could fit in the box. And because my treatment was so long, my chart had to have extra rows added – all of which were covered in stickers as I counted the days until my final visit to the hospital.

Throughout the radiotherapy I felt quite well – apart from a bit of a sore throat. I was given liquid paracetamol and Calpol, which I love! When I was little and Lee was ill I would queue up behind him and ask for some Calpol as well, and I would ask to lick the spoon even though I wasn't ill. That's how much I love Calpol.

Once I had finished my course of radiotherapy I was allowed to bring my chart and the mould of my face home, and I still have them. I keep them along with all kinds of things in a special memory box – like the Winnie the Pooh certificate I was given when my treatment was complete, the hospital wristband I wore during the operation, my signed school shirt and the good luck cards and letters my friends sent me.

I missed quite a bit of the beginning of secondary school because of the radiotherapy. I tried to go as much as possible, so I wasn't 'the new girl'. Sometimes I went in for just an hour, then Mum would pick me up to go to hospital for my treatment. A teacher was arranged to give me one-to-one tuition at home. I was only entitled to three hours a week. I didn't like the lessons – they were history lessons and I found them quite boring. The teacher only came for a few weeks. It wasn't the last I saw of him though – a year later he turned up at school as a support teacher!

December – rabbits!

On 1st December, the day of my last radiotherapy treatment, I presented a cheque for £2,500 to a representative from the Sargent Cancer Care charity. A friend of my auntie, Linda, had raised the money and asked me if I would like to choose a charity – Sargent Cancer Care seemed the most obvious one. In the photo I look like a little girl, skinny and flat-chested, with my hair in a bob – I've certainly changed since then.

I'd wanted my ears pierced since I was about eight, and Mum and Linda had said that my cousin Megan and I could have them done in the summer holidays before going to secondary school. When it got to the summer holidays though, I'd had my operation, and was then told I needed radiotherapy. I couldn't have them done because I'd had the mask made of my face and ears for the treatment, and I wouldn't be able to fit the mask on if I then had studs in my ears. It was really horrible, and the worst thing was that Megan still had her ears pierced in the holidays and I had to go along to watch! I had my ears pierced the day after my radiotherapy finished, and it was the thing that helped me through my treatment, because I knew I had that to look forward to.

I was given two rabbits, a present to cheer me up during my treatment. My dad built a hutch for them in the garden and my uncle built a huge run – three metres by two metres – which meant that if I wanted to catch them I had to climb into the run with them. Nutmeg and Sage came from a rabbit rescue centre – but I changed Sage's name to Womble because he was grey and fluffy. Nutmeg was – obviously – nutmeg-coloured – brown with ginger specks.

Molly was especially fond of Nutmeg, and because Nutmeg was overweight (she was a big breed anyway), the vet advised us to let Molly chase her round the garden for exercise. Both the rabbit and the dog loved the game, although Molly was always a bit disappointed that Nutmeg refused to chase her back!

2002

More tests – and chickenpox!

Twenty months after I had completed my radiotherapy I started to feel a throbbing, aching pain at the base of my spine. Tablets didn't help. A scan revealed what the doctors called 'a shadow' and I was sent to King's College Hospital in London to have an angiogram, which meant having another general anaesthetic. As I was thirteen by this time, I was too old for a strawberry-smelling gas mask.

For an angiogram a fine, wiry tube with a tiny camera on the end is manoeuvred through your veins, inserted through a vein in the groin. Doctors operate the tiny camera by remote control and watch the images carefully on a special television to make sure there is nothing suspicious or unusual. I felt the cold, uncomfortable sensation as the anaesthetic worked its way up my arm but I quickly fell asleep.

I remember waking up from the anaesthetic and Mum being beside me. I wasn't allowed to walk around for six hours after the procedure was completed as the cut in my groin had to heal. At one point, just after I had woken up, a nurse came over and whipped back the sheet to check the wound. I was thinking, 'Do you mind, you're flashing my bits there!' I really needed a pee but stubbornly held it in as I was determined not to pee in a pot.

The angiogram didn't show up anything unusual.

But the pain was still there, so about a month later I went back to the Royal Marsden Hospital in Surrey. I had been told before that I had a rare type of cancer and that it was unlikely to reseed, so I wasn't too worried. I was put under anaesthetic and a long needle was inserted into my spine for a lumbar puncture. I'm extremely glad that I knew nothing about it. The needle was used to withdraw some of the fluid that travels up and down my spine and round my brain. By checking the fluid and by measuring the speed at which it moved, the doctors could find out what was wrong with me. The lumbar puncture also showed there was nothing unusual, but there was still a shadow on my spine and I was still in pain, so everybody was worried. I was booked to have an exploratory operation at King's College Hospital at the end of July 2002.

Once again, I missed the end-of-term fun, including a Year 9 class trip to a theme park in France. Missing that bothered me more than the operation. Because I was older I was beginning to understand more of what was happening. I was worried, but I was more anxious than scared.

During the operation Chris Chandler cut a little trap door in my spine to get to the problem. I can't remember which hat he wore this time. The first thing he found was enlarged blood vessels so he decided against doing anything further because – as he explained to me later – if he'd cut one of the vessels I might have bled to death. He told us that it looked like something called an AVM (arterio venous malformation). When Mum looked at my back after the operation, she got a bit of a shock. My scar was in the middle of my back, and she thought they had operated in the wrong place because the pain I had been getting was at the base of my spine. It was the right place though!

The day I was coming out of hospital a teacher from the hospital school came round the ward. Other days she had passed by me, but that day she asked if I wanted to go to the school. I really didn't want to, but Mum had a migraine and made me go. She lay down in my bed while I went to the school. I really didn't want to be there. We were due to leave the hospital in a few hours, and I thought I had got away with not going to the school. There were a couple of other children in the room too. I was given a sheet of maths questions. I'm not really into maths, and didn't properly understand the questions, so it was a good job that the teacher had left the answer book next to me with the right page open!

I went back to school in the last week of term before breaking up for the summer holidays. For the Year 9s it was something called 'enrichment week', where you do all sorts of different activities from t'ai chi and baking to crafts and bookmark making. One activity was to go on a three-mile walk. I was advised not to do it, but I insisted. So a week after my operation, I walked over three miles through fields and woods. My back did hurt a bit, but I was glad I did it. It turned out to be quite fun because I was with my friends and we just chatted.

In the summer holiday we hired a coach to go to Chessington World of Adventures with lots of friends and family. I went with Rachel and Nicola. There was only one problem: I wasn't allowed to go on any of the rides because I had had my operation a few weeks earlier. The only ride I was allowed on was the spinning tea cups, and a boat that went up and down. I spent the majority of the time in the gift shop. One ride Nic and Rach went on was a rollercoaster. It had a really long queue, and I wasn't allowed to stand with them. I stood in the gift shop for over an hour, and ended up buying a stress ball to get my frustration out!

A few days later a swelling appeared around my scar which meant fluid was leaking inside. I went back to the hospital to have it drained. I felt dizzy after it had been done and was sick so I had to lie down for a while before going home. As soon as it was drained, it filled back up again. I used to push the bottom of it, and the top would bulge out. It was horrible! I was told to return to King's College Hospital for more surgery to find out what the problem was.

On the morning of the operation I noticed a few spots on my belly. It took three or four doctors to decide that I had caught chickenpox! I was then rushed into a room of my own so that I didn't infect any of the other children in the ward. The operation was cancelled. It was frustrating because I wanted to find out what the problem was and to have it fixed, but at the same time I remember being relieved not to be having another operation.

I was moved to Kent and Canterbury Hospital, where the swelling in my back was drained again and a pressure bandage was put on. I had a drip in each hand – one to stop the chickenpox from getting worse and the other to stop the itching. Late one night one of the drips stopped working and had to be replaced with another in my wrist. I remember crying because it was so painful. Mum had gone home for the night and I felt really lonely. I stayed in hospital for a week – I had to wait for the very last spot to scab over. It took ages and I was really bored. I wasn't allowed any visitors, in case they caught chickenpox, and I had to stay in my room.

I remember thinking I would try and go for a walk, but decided against it in case I got caught. I was so happy when we thought that the last spot had scabbed over but when the nurse took the bandage off my back, one last spot was revealed which wasn't yet ready. That meant another two days of waiting. I knew that everyone was out having fun in the summer holidays. I missed seeing and chatting to my friends. Linda's dog had four puppies while I was in hospital and I really wanted to see them. Mum knew how desperate I was and because they were born overnight she left me a photo and a note for when I woke up in the morning. But by that time I was so keen to be home that they made me feel even worse because I wanted to hold one of the puppies so much.

It ended on a positive note though. When the bandage came off, my back was fine and the doctors decided that I didn't need an operation after all. With having a pressure bandage on and lying down a lot in hospital reading magazines, the problem had sorted itself out! At least some good came out of it!

I was still getting pain in my back months later, so I went to King's for another lumbar puncture. I was awake for this one. I had to curl in the foetal position on a bed. There was a 'Where's Wally?' poster on the wall to distract children from what was happening to them. They told me to try and find Wally. By the time they had got out all the equipment, and wiped my back with the sterile stuff, I'd found Wally, and the lumbar puncture hadn't even started yet! I started crying then because I was so upset I had already found him! It was painful and really uncomfortable, but luckily it only lasted four or five minutes. It still didn't show what was wrong.

Devastating December

It was about 10.30 p.m. and I had been out to post the neighbours' Christmas cards. I came back into the house and Mum went into the living-room and shut the door because she was hanging the Christmas cards on the back of it. As I went to walk upstairs, I felt a sharp pain in my head and that is all I remember until I woke up on the floor with my head thumping.

Because I was so ill for much of the next few months, I'll let some other people tell their version of events, starting with my mum, who kept a diary for me so that when I recovered – and she always believed that I would recover – she could fill in the gaps for me.

Saturday 14th December

When I shut the living-room door I heard a bang, then you making funny noises. I thought you were teasing the dog, so I ignored you and started to put Christmas cards on the back of the door. When you didn't stop I opened the door to shout at you to go to bed. That's when I realised something was wrong. I regret not opening the door sooner but I know those minutes wouldn't have made any difference. Your eyes were rolling; you were shaking and didn't really understand me.

I phoned the children's ward at Kent and Canterbury Hospital, as they know your history, and they asked if I could bring you in right away. I thought I could but I couldn't lift you off the floor, so I phoned for an ambulance.

I had gone up three stairs before collapsing without any warning. The noises Mum had heard were me having a fit. When I regained consciousness after a few minutes I was aware of being sore – I had banged my nose on the radiator and my head on the floor – and of the lights hurting my eyes. I was shaking uncontrollably. I pulled Molly's dog bed under my head for a pillow and Mum brought me my duvet because I was cold. Mum phoned the ambulance. I don't know how long it took them to come. I think I was drifting in and out of consciousness. Molly was beside me the whole time and I was stroking her. She was shaking.

It was probably twenty minutes until the ambulance came but it felt much longer.

I tried to stand but couldn't, so the ambulancemen put me on a stretcher. They wrapped me in a blanket and were about to lift me when I was sick all over the floor and on the blanket. I was more confused than scared. All I remember in the ambulance was that I kept trying to pull the oxygen mask off and the ambulanceman kept putting it back on. It was annoying me and all I wanted to do was sleep.

I was taken to Accident and Emergency. It was Saturday night, so it was full of drunks. I don't remember much as I was mostly unconscious. But at some point I remember a nurse saying, 'Nicole, Nicole,' and the drunk man in the next cubicle, thinking the nurse was saying, 'Cold, cold,' said, 'Cold? Cold? I'm bloody freezing.'

* * *

After being in A & E for over an hour we went to the children's ward. You just wanted to sleep, touching your head, saying it was sore. After you had been examined by a few doctors, they decided to keep you in overnight and phone King's College Hospital in the morning. I was told to go home and pack a bag. Linda, who had met us at the hospital earlier, dropped me at home at 5.30 a.m. I cleared up your sick, packed a bag for both of us for a couple of days, then got to bed at 6.30 a.m.

I remember waking up smiling because I was in the room with Winnie the Pooh and Eeyore painted on the walls. My other stays at Kent and Canterbury Hospital had been in the rooms with Postman Pat, Paddington Bear or mermaids on the wall but I had always wanted to be in the Winnie the Pooh room. So that was why I was happy! It took me a few seconds to remember that I was in hospital, and a second longer to realise that I must be really ill if I was in this room, the room nearest to the reception desk, where the poorly patients go.

I don't remember much about the tests and scans I then had, which is probably a good thing in the circumstances.

Sunday 15th December

Kent and Canterbury Hospital phoned me at 8 a.m. to say they had spoken to your doctors at King's College Hospital and they wanted you to have a brain scan. I was back at the hospital in twenty minutes. The results of the scan were sent to King's by computer and as soon as they saw them they wanted you there right away. You were being sick all the time and your head was really sore. Nanny came in to see you before we were taken to London by ambulance. As well as the ambulance staff, we had a nurse and a doctor just in case anything went wrong, then it was flashing lights all the way. You were taken straight to the high dependency unit (HDU).

I'd always wanted to go in an ambulance with the siren on and the lights flashing but as I was dipping in and out of consciousness, I don't remember the journey. In fact I can't remember much about the next few months. I wasn't in control of what was happening to me and I still find that upsetting. Reading Mum's diary shows me how much I missed, and yet it was all about me.

You have been sick all day and we have to leave you in the dark for bed-rest but you can't sleep as your head is thumping. The scan showed that you had a haemorrhage on the surface of your brain, which could have come from your AVM. Chris Chandler is in tomorrow so he should cheer you up.

Monday 16th December

Chris was not pleased to see you under these circumstances and has advised you to have an angiogram. This is to determine if the bleed came from your AVM.

Your head is still sore and you can't get to sleep – you know how noisy children's wards are. You're still being sick and haven't eaten anything since Saturday. You are finding it hard to drink from a cup so you're using a straw.

I remember waking up and saying I needed to be out of hospital by Wednesday because I was going ice skating with my school. I didn't realise how ill I was and genuinely thought I would get out in time.

Tuesday 17th December

Nanny and Linda have come to see you. You have been moved to a room on your own, so you can be in the dark and can get peace and quiet. The results from yesterday couldn't prove that it was your AVM that caused the bleeding.

At 2 p.m. the doctor was trying to take a blood sample and you had another fit that lasted eight minutes. Chris Chandler was worried you were having another haemorrhage so sent you for a CT scan right away. These results showed that you hadn't bled again. At least this room is nice and quiet for you. I can sleep beside your bed here. That wasn't allowed in the HDU. You've been put on a high dose of Phenytoin to stop you having fits. You're still being sick and don't want to eat.

The next thing I remember is hearing a man with a Scottish accent sitting on the end of my bed, talking to me. I was totally confused. It wasn't until I opened my eyes that I saw a blurry version of my dad. I tried to speak but my words were slurred.

Probably one of the last things I saw was my dad leaving and Father Christmas arriving and giving me a present, but it is all so muddled in my mind. What I remember is that I was tired, I couldn't move and all I wanted to do was sleep.

Wednesday 18th December

At 7 a.m. you had another fit. This time they took you for an MRI scan. You were there for one and a half hours as they scanned your brain and spine. We are still unsure where the haemorrhage has come from. Chris now wants to do a lumbar puncture but you're not happy about that. You're really drowsy and finding it hard to see. You couldn't count how many fingers Chris held up. Your scans have been sent to Oxford for other experts to examine.

Chris took me to a side room and said he was really worried about you. He's not sure what he is dealing with, and warned me that you could get worse before you get better. You are back in HDU so they can keep a closer eye on you. Dad flew down for the day to see you. He got a bit of a shock when he saw how bad you were. You couldn't see him very well. You told him he wasn't as fat and bald as you remembered, but that he had two heads! He flew back to Scotland at 4 o'clock.

Thursday 19th December

You're not being sick as much but you still won't eat. The light hurts your eyes so you keep them shut. They are still taking blood tests and they have given you another angiogram. Chris is going on holiday at the weekend and you're quite sad about that. He has asked another doctor to look after you. To cheer you up I said, 'Never mind, the new doctor might wear loud ties like Chris.' And you replied, 'And suspenders.' I think you meant his braces. Well, I hope you did!

Friday 20th December

Hardly talking to me at all and you're not able to see anything. Linda and Lee are here to see you today. You knew they were here and you waved to Lee but didn't talk to him. Nurses are finding it hard to get a vein in your hand for the blood tests, so they're trying your feet but not having much luck. Linda and Lee left at 2 o'clock and as we were changing your bed you had another fit – only a small one, two minutes long. You had another brain scan. You have not had another bleed which is good, but the pressure in your head is high. They have increased the dose of Phenytoin again. You still won't eat anything so they have put a tube up your nose and into your stomach. The dietician has worked out a diet appropriate to your body weight. You are too weak and couldn't get out of bed to go to the toilet so you now have a catheter.

Saturday 21st December

I got a shock when I saw you this morning at 7 o'clock. You have scratched your face and the inside of your eye trying to pull the tube out of your nose. You don't understand me any more and you're not talking. You can't swallow tablets so they are crushing some and others are in liquid form and fed through your tubes. You can't use a straw now so I'm squirting Ribena into your mouth with a syringe. It seems you have a urine infection, so we sent a sample off to the lab. It came back negative. Your urine is not draining away properly. You haven't moved your legs all day.

Once you're asleep every night I go along the corridor to my bed. I can turn my phone on there. I write all the text messages you receive on the back of an envelope. You got twelve last night. Here are a few of them:

Hi nic we r al misin u so much rite now. I hope u get beta soon. We al luv u so so much. Loada letas r on da way 2 u. I hope u r home agen soon. Luv u rach xx

Hi nic I hope u r ok. We miss u so much, plz get beta soon. I love u 2 bits n we r al thinking of u. love u chez xxxx

Hi nic! Hope u r ok and get beter real soon hopefully b4 xmas! Sorry 2 hear u have 2 b in then. Mr Marsh has posted sum letes & cards 4 u. hope 2 c u soon love nic xxx

Hi nic hw r u? I hope u r arite n gt beta soon. Im finkin of u al da time n cant wait til u cm ome. Im sorry. Love u loadz kez xxxxxxxxx tims a million more!

Imagine what it was like for Mum having to read text messages like that when I was so ill. Although everything was happening to me, I think it was worse for her having to watch me go through it.

Sunday 22nd December

You were restless all last night and your tummy is starting to swell, the catheter is blocked, and they keep trying to flush it. Your eye is really sore where you scratched it. Linda and Megan up to see you, Megan a bit shocked and didn't know what to say but helped give you a drink with the syringe. Doctors really worried about you and still don't know what's wrong and why you are getting worse. Called a surgeon up at 2 a.m. tried to get the catheter out but it's faulty. He said it could wait until the morning. Your tummy is really swollen now, sent another urine sample off.

At 3 a.m. a doctor from Guy's Hospital explained that

*he thought it could be the start of another tumour. He wasn't sure and wanted to put you on steroids. At this time in the morning I couldn't concentrate on what he was saying. Everybody has a different opinion on what they think is wrong with you. I didn't get to bed until 4 o'clock. All I could see was this man's moustache and dickie bow and the words **tumour tumour tumour**. Where is Chris Chandler when you need him?*

I can't think of a way to describe being in a coma. I was awake, but couldn't move or speak or communicate with people. People talked to me and I tried to talk back, but I couldn't. I was scared in case they thought I was dead.

I had weird dreams as well. I once dreamt I was a chicken! Now I realise that the dream happened at the same time as my tummy swelled up. I dreamt I was a chicken trying to lay an egg. I was in a weird chicken house and I was hiding at the back of it so I wasn't made into a chicken nugget like all my chicken friends. I started to feel sorry for chickens, knowing what pain they go through laying their eggs!

The next day I dreamt that Mum was sticking an apple core up my nose but it was the nurse putting in the feeding tube because I wasn't eating. I kept trying to pull it out.

I even thought someone had put me in the washing

machine before killing me and burying me under the patio. I have no idea why I was dreaming these things. Perhaps the most bizarre dream was about a race on the beach with Ann Widdecombe. And the worst bit was that she won! The next night she chased me with a knife. My dreams were all a bit gruesome.

Monday 23rd December

You're not talking, drinking, moving, can't see, fed through a drip, faulty catheter making your tummy swollen, an eye infection and now the results say you have a urine infection. Today for the first time I cried. It is a year today since Auntie Eileen died and I can see your body shutting down and giving up like hers did. I'm frightened. The nurses have been measuring your tummy with a tape measure to record how big you've been getting through the night. When a doctor did the early ward rounds he was mad when he saw your tummy. When he was told the catheter wasn't done last night he told them to do it right away, and they did.

I met the doctor who is looking after you while Chris is away. He is really nice and looks like he will get things done. He ordered someone from Guy's Hospital to come over to give their opinion. Linda and Julie came up to see you; I got upset when I saw them. Julie took me for lunch while Linda tried to get some answers. When the doctor came over from Guy's he recognised us from a visit to the Mary Sheridan Centre. He read your notes and examined you, then suggested lumbar punctures to relieve the pressure in your head. Also that they measure brain activity with electrodes to see if you were having any mini fits. You were given a lumbar puncture right away; the pressure was way too high. You didn't move, you didn't feel a thing.

None of the doctors could work out what was wrong with me but they were sure that it wasn't another tumour. At one point they even checked to see if I was brain dead. They connected wires to my head with the other end of the wires linked up to a machine. They did tests such as pinching me on both sides of my body to see if I responded.

I did.

Tuesday 24th December

Today they put fourteen electrodes on your head and watched your brain activity on the computer screen. I was asked to talk to you to see if you reacted. You slept right through it. You had another lumbar puncture done this morning; again you slept through but you were restless. You kept grabbing at the oxygen mask they gave you yesterday because you're finding it hard to breathe. Also, you're grabbing your tummy as if something is wrong. Dad flew down again from Scotland. He is staying in London with Lee over Christmas. They have both come in today.

You had another lumbar puncture at 3 o'clock. You didn't like this one and put up a bit of a fight. The doctor said to let him know if there is any change in you. The only change is that you now push my hand away when I put the cream in your eye to help your infection. You have scratches on your nose, forehead and in your ears. We spend all day moving your hands away from your face and telling you the oxygen mask has to stay on, and that you can't pull the feeding tube out either.

At 7 p.m. you tried again to take the mask off. I thought I heard you say, "Get it off." Not sure if I heard you right so I took the mask off and asked you what you had just said. You then said, 'Drink.' I was so happy as this was the first time you'd spoken since Friday and I ran around the ward telling everyone. I was too emotional to phone home. Lee did it for me. Everyone cried, but they were happy tears and we hoped this was a sign that you were getting better. It's the best Christmas present ever and I went to bed happy.

* * *

I vaguely remember Christmas Day. I was definitely a bit better, but as you will read from Mum's next diary entry, I wasn't a model patient.

Wednesday 25th December

MERRY CHRISTMAS!

When I came in this morning at 7 o'clock, you had taken the mask off and told them to pull the food tube out as you feel better and will eat normally today. You were propped up in bed – lovely to see you like that.

Looks like you have had a stroke while you have been in a coma for the last few days as you are finding it difficult to move the right side of your body. Every time you want to move, I have to do it for you. I need the nurses to help me. If they are busy and can't do it straight away, you shout, 'Come on, you people, move me!'

I explain that it's Christmas Day, describe the ward and all its decorations and tell you that Santa left presents at the end of your bed. When your nurse asks you if you know what day it is you tell her, 'I'm not stupid, you know!'

When Lee and Dad came in it was Christmas kisses all round! Dad had brought you presents but you said you would open them when you got better. I have to write down everything that you eat. Today you had one spoonful of Coco Pops for breakfast, lunch was half a syringe of tomato soup, so by 7 p.m. they had to put the food tube back in. You can't move your legs but you're starting to move your toes. Everybody says to give you time.

Catheter blocked again, they have to flush it. The nurse was trying to wake you up and you told her to 'bugger off'. Lee thought this was very funny. I'm so glad you've got your voice back but you're not the same child that fell asleep last week. I've spent all day apologising for you.

You got one text message today:

Merry chrimbo babe hope you feel better soon hope you got loadza prezzies can't w8 2 c u. loadza luv Olivia xxxxxxxxxx

I hope you understand these messages, I'm writing them down exactly as they come in. I'm even counting how many kisses. All this text malarkey is new to me.

Thursday 26th December

You want to turn over and move all the time in bed, but can't, as your arms and legs feel very heavy. You get annoyed if you're not moved right away. You try to do it yourself but end up throwing your legs over the side of the bed, which means that you flash your bottom, so I can't leave you. You tell me, 'It's not a bottom, it's an *arse.' I whisper, 'Sshhh, you can't say that,' so you make up a song and sing, 'Dumb-arse, dumb-arse, dumb-arse,' in a loud voice . . . A lovely nurse called Marlene has been great and always sits with you if I do have to leave your side. You are slipping in and out of a coma all the time, but for the odd five minutes that you are with us, you still find time to shout at the nurses.*

The first thing I wanted to know when I woke from the coma was which band – the girls or the boys – had won *Popstars the Rivals*. I had been watching the programme every Saturday night before my haemorrhage and wanted to know whether Girls Aloud or One True Voice had got to Number 1.

Honestly, I was much more interested in finding that out than discovering what was wrong with me.

Friday 27th December

Today we found out why you can't move. You have had a stroke. Your whole right side is paralysed. You've also had a Bell's palsy so your face is twisted, and you can't shut your right eye. Your lovely smile is all lopsided too. God, what else can go wrong? You don't do things by half. It's all or nothing.

You're complaining that you can't see anything, but as you are asleep for hours on end, we are concentrating on all your other problems for the moment. Chris comes back on Monday; so as long as we can get through this weekend, I'll be happy.

I remember waking up and everything being black. At first I thought it must be night-time but then I realised I couldn't see a thing, not even the usual shadows that you can normally see at night. I just knew something was seriously wrong. I don't think I panicked or felt scared. I just tried to understand why everything was black.

Monday 30th December

Chris Chandler came back today. He took a long time to read through your notes. He then talked to Nanny, Linda and me about what he thought had gone wrong. He sent you for another MRI scan. It looked better than your last one, as the blood clot had got smaller. Couldn't see if there was any damage to your eyes; all the nerves were swollen and this was also affecting your legs etc. He says things should go back to normal in time. 'Tumour doctor' back and still wants to put you on steroids, but Chris is convinced it's not a tumour. It's the AVM. He arranged for an ophthalmologist to look at your eyes. Apparently the pupils are not reacting to light.

Here is one of the seven texts that you got today:

Hey Nic, I'm not sure wat 2 say but I want u 2 no u r 1 of my best m8s. I hope u get beta as I love u so much. We r al really worried and miss u. love chez

Sometimes it's hard to read these messages to you as they're getting a bit emotional.

Tuesday 31st December

It's New Year's Eve today and you had a full spine and brain MRI scan which lasted one and a half hours. You put up a bit of a fight, which isn't like you. They had to strap you in to keep you still. You can be so horrible to people. I'm now wondering whether you've got brain damage. Results show there was pressure on the optic nerve, so you might not get full vision back, but then again you might – only time will tell. Another ophthalmologist is coming to see you tomorrow. The scan also showed you've had a paralysis down the whole of your right side. There was severe damage to the blood supply. They explained that this has been happening slowly to you, which is why every day you've been getting worse.

New Year's Day 2003

Not much change in you apart from being able to move your arms a couple of inches off the bed. It's a good sign. Had a text from Nicola, who's just back from Lanzarote and didn't know you were in hospital. I had to text her back and explain the situation. I can't talk to anyone on the phone – it's too emotional. I normally get Marlene or another nurse to talk to whoever is on the phone.

Thursday 2nd January 2003

The ophthalmologist said there was no surface damage, so we just have to wait and see how well the nerves repair themselves. This gives us a bit of hope.

Hi nic and her mum. I hope u r feelin bit beta. We al missed u 2day bac at skool. I sent a card and leta I duno if u got them tho. Hope I c u soon. Luv loads rach x

Friday 3rd January

Blood test, urine test and a Zenon CT scan today. This is a new one that we haven't been through before, so I can't reassure you that it will be OK. You're very restless and don't want it done as you're fed up with all these tests and drugs you have to take. I find out you have to wear a mask and they pump 'steam' round your face, but you have to stay still while it's happening. It's difficult trying to explain things to you as you still haven't got any sight back. I have to wear a heavy lead apron, which makes it difficult to bend over the table as I have to keep pulling your hands away from your face because you keep trying to pull the mask off.

Saturday 4th January

You ate two chips today – the first solid food you've had for weeks! Then this afternoon I noticed a few spots on your tummy, they were appearing before my eyes. Panic set in and a nurse, a doctor, then a dermatologist was called. The rash spread rapidly to your arms, legs and face. They stopped some of your drugs and gave you antihistamine to stop the itch. You are depressed today as yet another thing is going wrong. You cry that you want to go home and see Molly, open Christmas presents and be normal. I cry with you because if the doctors don't know what is wrong with you, how can I reassure you that you will be fine?

Sunday 5th January

When I saw you this morning I got a shock. The spots are covering your whole body – your ears, scalp, palm of your hands, in between your toes, everywhere. You also have ulcers in your mouth and it looks like your lips are swollen. You are so hot and itchy. After three attempts they managed to get a line in your hand, but you are so upset and depressed that I'm frightened you'll have another fit. They think it is the anti-fit drug you are having an allergic reaction to, so they've taken you off it. They have even phoned Chris at home.

Monday 6th January

You look as though you have been stung by a thousand bees. Your mouth, lips and throat are so swollen and you can't talk. There are ulcers all around your tongue, and round your mouth. Lips are double the usual size and the rash has blurred into one mass of red blotches. You are so hot and itchy. I have to put petroleum jelly on you three times a day. As I put a blob of it on you, it slides off like hot butter. A sort of lilo filled with ice-cold air was placed over you, to help to reduce your high temperature. Chris Chandler arrived and could only shake his head. 'Don't

worry,' he told me, 'I'll get the best team to look after her.'
It turns out that his wife is a dermatologist at the hospital.
She came in with a team of people, examined you and
explained she thought you were having what is called a
Stevens-Johnson reaction to the anti-fit drug, Phenytoin.
They would have to do a skin biopsy to make sure. This
meant numbing a tiny patch on your stomach. They used
what I can only describe as an apple corer. It was the size
of the lead in a pencil. This was pushed into your skin,
and came out with a piece of your skin in it. You needed
two stitches afterwards and although you knew we were
doing it, I thought you coped really well.

Dr McCormick came into hospital to introduce himself
to the nurses before he leaves Kent and Canterbury
Hospital to start his new job here next month. He came
straight into the HDU, took one look at you, and gave me
a big hug. It felt as if he couldn't say anything to reassure
me, so had to hug me to get the message across. It
worked, I cried that night. This must be the end.

Linda and Julie here. They were shocked to see how
bad you were. You have to wave and use hand signals to
communicate. Your mouth and throat are sore and they
have given you a high dose of antibiotics to combat the
infection, which makes you drowsy. You aren't as hot but
still look red and sore. We have to put tablets on your
tongue, to help the ulcers. I have to spray water into your

mouth as your saliva has dried up. It is sore for you to open your mouth. I could only spray twice today and the tablets didn't dissolve because your mouth is so dry. You slept for five hours this afternoon. I was sure that as soon as I left your bed you'd wake up, so I didn't have my dinner until 8.30 p.m. – when you woke up. Then you fell asleep again until 1.00 a.m., so I wouldn't go to bed until after that. I thought you would wonder where I was, as you were very disorientated.

Wednesday 8th January

Nanny and Auntie Jean travelled in the snow to see us today. Nanny quite upset to see you like this. Again you just waved, as you couldn't talk. A consultant ophthalmologist has seen you today and can't promise that you will ever get your sight back. He will see you again on Friday.

Thursday 9th January

Your tongue is white and furry and covered in ulcers. Your gums are red-raw and your lips and throat are swollen and sore. You keep crying today, which hurts, and you

*whisper, 'Why me? I just want to be normal.' It's
heartbreaking to watch and you know I'm crying, as you
keep shaking your head, wagging your finger, and
pointing to your eyes, as if to say, 'Don't cry, Mum.'*

Friday 10th January

*Chris Chandler's wife came back today with her team of
dermatologists. She is happy with your skin condition and
says that we caught it just in time. One more dose of
Phenytoin could have been fatal. You will have to wear a
medic alert bracelet from now on, so that you are never
given this drug again.*

While I was in King's College Hospital I was asked if
there was anything I wanted. I was seriously ill and
pretty miserable. I said I missed Molly, so Linda took
Molly to the vet to get a letter to say that Molly was
healthy and gentle – perfect for a hospital visit. We
checked with all the children on the ward to make sure
they weren't scared of dogs, or allergic to them, and
luckily nobody ever was.

Seeing Molly that Friday was one of the only times
I was happy. And after that, Linda brought her every
Friday, often bringing Lee too. The first time Molly was

scared. I was in a strange place and I probably looked and smelt different. And I didn't sound the same either, because of the stroke. I don't even think she knew it was me. But Molly was really happy to see Mum – she hadn't seen either of us for four weeks.

I gave Molly her Christmas presents. She wouldn't sit on my bed because it was spongy and she didn't like the feel of it. She sat on Mum's lap eating a cowhide shoe I'd given her. I tried to get her to go under my duvet, like she used to do at home, but she didn't want to.

Linda brought Molly in to see you today for the first time. She kept jumping off the bed on to my lap which upset you. The hospital say that she can come back again as she is so well behaved.

Monday 13th January

You had the two biopsy stitches out today. The physiotherapists have decided that it's time to see if you can sit up as you have been lying flat ever since you came into hospital – a month ago. You only last two minutes as you are weak and in pain. You are now in the main ward which means I can sleep beside you at night. Before, I would sit with you until you fell asleep, sometimes as late as 2.30 a.m. I'd then go to my room, which I often had to share with the parents of other sick children, write down the text messages that had come in for you, then try to get to sleep so I could be with you at 7 a.m. when you woke up again. At least now I will be with you day and night. You asked the nurses if they could take the food tube out. You have promised to eat. You are on a strict warning that if you don't, it will go straight back in.

Tuesday 14th January

I had to register you as blind today. A very, very sad day.

Mum was told to fill in a BD8 form to register me blind, as she had to accept now that I wouldn't get my sight back. At the time I didn't understand what it meant. As a registered blind person I get certain advantages such as disabled parking and half-price TV licence.

Wednesday 15th January

Nanny and Sue came in today. Sue made you laugh a few times which was good. You ate a few Frosties which is a good sign if you want to eat properly again. You had an

MRI scan to look for any changes. The cannula in your hand is causing problems as usual.

Thursday 16th January

You're still not eating, so the feeding tube has been put back in. You gagged on it. You're more conscious of what's happening to you. Physio still hurts all down your right side when they make you sit up.

Friday 17th January

You were sick twice during the night. Luckily it was over the other side of the bed and not on me, now that I'm sleeping on the floor beside you. You say the food tube hurts you as you swallow, but they don't believe you when you say you will eat. They have found you an electric bed to help you sit up slowly. But it doesn't have any sides on it yet, so it isn't safe enough to use it. You need the sides up because you are disorientated. We have a baby on this open ward who cries day and night. Poor thing, I know she's not well either but it disturbs everyone's sleep.

Saturday 18th January

You wanted to use the electric bed so you could sit up. Propping you up with pillows doesn't work. You still haven't got much control over your body. If you lie on your side I have to put pillows behind you, so you don't roll on to your back. I still have to move your legs as they feel very heavy. When you move one leg you can't move the other. You promised the nurse you would be OK in the electric bed with no sides, so we swapped beds. This wasn't easy because you couldn't help us and your body feels like a dead weight. We had to have three nurses, one for your head, one for your feet and one for your body, to slide you over on a sheet from one bed to another. You had been in bed no longer than an hour when you tried to move your leg. It fell over the side, and because you couldn't stop yourself, your body followed. I caught your top half before you reached the floor. You're now back in your old bed with the sides up.

Monday 20th January

You keep complaining of a pain in your leg, so they gave you a scan (like a baby monitor) to see if you have a DVT. Luckily you don't. We were asked today if we want to move back to Kent and Canterbury Hospital.

Mrs Winston from Barton Court phoned to say that they would give your girls the day off on Thursday and a teacher would bring them up to hospital to see you. First time you've smiled in a long time even if it is still lopsided with the Bell's palsy.

Tuesday 21st January

A psychiatrist came today to see if you wanted to talk to her about how depressed you are feeling. You told me you felt better and didn't want to talk to her. When she came back at 3 p.m. you pretended you were asleep. Chris Chandler wants another MRI scan done today. He will then talk to me about the results. Good! I feel a bit left out these days – when the doctors do their rounds in the morning they don't come to your bed any more. I hear all the other children being told they can go home as they are much better. They never know what will happen to you day by day, so they don't make any comment. We just get a smile and a hello, and then they move on to the next patient.

Wednesday 22nd January

Nanny and Auntie Jean saw a big difference in you when they visited. You showed them how, with a lot of help, you can sit up with your legs over the bed. It was only for two minutes because of the pain in your back.

Chris Chandler asked me to come into a side room tonight, so he could explain your MRI results. I thought this was a bit strange as we normally talk at your bedside so you can hear us. He looked really upset and couldn't talk to begin with. Eventually he admitted that it was bad news. The scan shows you have an aggressive tumour, not an AVM, at the base of your spine. There are lots of little ones at the top of your spine and around your brain. Now that the swelling is reducing they are able to assess better what's going on. It's too risky to operate so chemotherapy is the only option, but Chris is not sure if your body can tolerate it because it has been through so much already. Before any decisions are made, a biopsy will be necessary. I know he was trying to tell me that the outcome wasn't going to be good, but I didn't want to hear it.

It was such devastating news that everything in the room went quiet and I got a buzzing sound in my ears. I could see Chris's lips moving but couldn't hear a sound. I started to think of silly things, like you haven't opened your Christmas presents yet, and it's your birthday in two weeks' time. Will you make it until then? Chris wants to tell you about the biopsy tonight but I know you are excited about The Girls coming tomorrow, so I ask him to wait and he agreed.

I cried my eyes out when he left the room. Marlene held me for about ten minutes until I stopped sobbing. I tried to be cheery when I came back to your bed but I'm sure you knew something was wrong.

The food tube has been taken out again, so I have to record how much you eat each day.

Thursday 23rd January

I couldn't sleep last night. You wanted your hair washed this morning, so we moved your bed into the middle of the ward so we could get behind it. We then put a baby bath on the floor and sheets under your head. One nurse held your head and neck, another one poured the water and I was on shampoo duty. You have such long thick hair that it took us twenty minutes and all the time I kept thinking, you will lose this hair if you have to have chemo.

I remember the day when Kerry, Charlotte, Rachel and Nicola came to visit. Mrs Winston, the deputy head teacher, had asked which of my friends I would like to see and Mr Gugenheim, our science teacher, drove them to the hospital in the school bus.

Mum washed my hair and blow-dried it, turning the ends under. I had the food drip removed so I didn't look too scary.

The Girls arrived at 11 a.m. While Mr Gugenheim parked the school bus I met The Girls. They were really nervous coming up in the lift. I explained to them that the rash was a bit better, the marks would eventually fade and your face was still twisted. They would have to put things in your hand and explain everything. We all held hands in the lift and I asked them to act as normal as they could. I said that you would just be so pleased that they had come to see you.

As soon as they saw you, there were cries of, 'Hi, Nicole!' and it was straight into school gossip. To see you giggling and smiling brought a lump to my throat.

We sent Mum and Mr Gugenheim off to the café because we didn't want them listening in to our conversations! The Girls had brought presents and cards and a huge grey bear wearing a T-shirt saying, 'We love you'. Lee had brought my Christmas presents for The Girls to the ward a few days earlier so we swapped presents – nearly a month late. We watched a video they'd made in which everybody in my class said, 'Hi!' We laughed a lot. In fact we were eventually told off for talking and giggling too loudly! Mum and Mr Gugenheim came back from the café about three times and we kept sending them away, saying we weren't ready. Eventually, after four hours and a long goodbye, The Girls left.

I had no idea at the time that Mum had been told the day before that it was very likely that I was going to die.

Mr Gugenheim and I spent most of the day in the canteen. He was the first person I told about the news I'd heard from Chris and I cried.

When we eventually persuaded The Girls that it was time to go, they said that you weren't as bad as they thought you would be. You slept for three hours when they'd left. You were exhausted. I was watching you sleep, thinking how your day was going to change tomorrow when Chris tells you about your tumour.

Friday 24th January

Linda, Lee and Molly cheered you up today. A nurse slipped up by talking about the biopsy. I was angry because I wanted Chris to explain it to you and I thought you would accept it better from him.

You were given liquid morphine today. It made you gag. I have asked for tablets next time. It took the pain away but you started to get some spots, so we've stopped it. Darren Hargraves, consultant paediatric oncologist from the Royal Marsden Hospital, came in to look at your scans today and give a second opinion.

You ate a spoonful of Frosties, a few chips with The Girls and half a glass of milk yesterday. It wasn't much, and it took a lot for you to do it. I know it's only the threat of the tube going back that's making you eat.

Sunday 26th January

It was difficult to lie to you all day. We had to give you a blood test, which is traumatic at the best of times. You wanted to know the reason for it. I can't remember what excuse we used but luckily the nurse did it first time. I also had to secretly sign the consent form.

There is no eating or drinking after 6 a.m. As you haven't been eating or drinking much in the past few days, the nil by mouth rule isn't going to be a problem.

I promise, Nicole, I will never lie to you again.

Monday 27th January

Chris came in early this morning and by 8 a.m. he was sitting beside you explaining that you have an aggressive tumour and that he will have to do a biopsy. You were very upset and I had to talk you into having it done. I explained why I hadn't told you sooner, and you agreed it would have upset you and made you worry all this time. By 9 a.m. you were on your way to theatre. For some reason, after the anaesthetic started to work I was really nervous and had a lump in my throat when I kissed you goodbye. Chris put his arm round me as I left the room and told me things would be fine. I always believe him, so I hoped so. The operation lasted three hours, so by the time Chris came to tell me you were OK I was feeling anxious. He said you'd lost a lot of blood through the AVM which is why everything took longer than planned. You feel dizzy, upset and complain that your foot is sore. You can't sleep because the morphine pump is stinging in one hand and you have a drip in the other hand that is hurting.

Tuesday 28th January

You get them to take the morphine pump out of your hand and the pain team come round to offer you a drug to take the pain away in your foot. *Yesterday's anaesthetic and today's drugs have made you hallucinate. You think the bed is moving and you are falling out. You look really frightened.*

Wednesday 29th January

Nanny and Linda saw a difference in you today. You feel a bit better and you can move your arms and legs a fraction off the bed.

Friday 31st January

We agreed that you are ready to go to Kent and Canterbury Hospital next week. It's much nearer for everyone to come and visit. It is snowing today and Lesley flew down from Scotland but couldn't get transport to the hospital because of the bad weather. She finally reached Canterbury at 2 a.m. and Linda will bring her here in the morning.

Saturday 1st February

Linda had a full car today – Nanny, Megan, Lesley and Molly. It's the first time that Lesley has seen you and considering all the stories she's been getting on the phone, she was very anxious. She said you looked better than she imagined. We had a nice surprise visit from Janice and Sean, my friends from Scotland. They had been in London for a dinner-dance last night. It was great to see them, albeit emotional. You find it very confusing when a lot of people talk at once. I'll need to remember that for the future. We have arranged for Lesley to stay in the hospital tonight as long as no other admissions need to use the parents' room.

Sunday 2nd February

Lesley was excited this morning because the girl she shared the room with was a Bon Jovi fan like her. So instead of sitting worrying all night, they talked about Bon Jovi until 2.30 a.m. We had a good day today. Lesley can talk for Scotland, so I had a rest. She has moaned at you so much about your eating that you reluctantly had something to eat.

Chris came in today, which was a surprise as you don't

69

normally see him at weekends. I thought he looked as
though he wanted to tell us something, but kept looking at
Lesley, as if he didn't want to spoil our weekend.

Monday 3rd February

This morning Laura Ireland, liaison nurse specialist, asked
me to go with her for a meeting with Chris and Dr
McCormick who started work here today. I knew we were
going to discuss the scan and biopsy results and it wasn't
going to be a pleasant meeting. I took a box of tissues
with me this time. With difficulty Chris explained that the
biopsy showed the original tumour had reseeded at the
base of your spine. The enlarged blood vessels had been
feeding off it, which is why Chris thought it was an AVM,
and the scan revealed that you had a splattering of small
tumours on your spine and brain. There's nothing else
they can do. He explained that they could only offer
chemotherapy to try and reduce the tumour, as surgery
isn't an option. He said that Darren Hargraves could talk
us through the chemotherapy treatment, once you'd
been told about the tumour. That's the bit that set me off.
Who was going to tell you that you have to go through the
trauma of chemotherapy, without a positive result?

I remember the day when I was told I had tumours all over my spine and brain. Mum had been taken to another room, which annoyed me because it felt as if I had been forgotten, or wouldn't be able to cope with the information. Without being told, I knew another tumour had been found and I had a funny feeling I had one on my brain.

When Mum came back to my bed, she was with Chris Chandler and a number of other doctors. I had Chris on one side and Mum and Dr McCormick on the other, and everyone else around the end of my bed. Mum told me later that it looked like a scene from Snow White and the Seven Dwarfs with my black hair sprawled out on the pillow. Mum had asked Chris to explain the results but he kept rubbing his face. Finally, he managed and I took it all in. I tried not to cry but couldn't help myself – the tears didn't last long though. They mentioned chemotherapy but I immediately said no. I was thirteen, I was naive, and my hair was important to me. I wanted to be in control of which treatments I would have.

The doctors were about to leave when Mum said, 'Could we just listen to what they have to say?'

'Fine,' I said, 'but there's no point.'

They then explained that I could have the chemotherapy in liquid or tablet form. I could be transferred to Kent and Canterbury Hospital for the treatment. So I said I'd think about it.

As soon as they had pulled the curtain round my bed I told Mum to go out and tell them that I would try the chemotherapy. I don't know what made me change my mind. Perhaps it was the sound of Mum's voice. And I just wanted to start feeling better.

Tuesday 4th February

They are making arrangements to transfer us tomorrow to Kent and Canterbury Hospital. They're trying to sort out the drugs and an electric bed. I have started packing. You wouldn't believe how many things you have gathered around this bed in the last few months. Linda has arranged for Blue, one of your favourite bands, to phone you this week. You can't believe it and every time your bedside phone rings, you laugh at my telephone voice.

Wednesday 5th February

When I left King's College Hospital that day I think Chris Chandler thought that it would be the last time he would see me. I suppose I owe everything to Chris.

Thank you, Chris.

Being ill wasn't all bad though! In fact it has some advantages . . .

I was a huge fan of Gareth Gates, and Linda arranged for him to send me his autograph, and he also sent me his CD.

She also arranged for Blue – one of my favourite bands – to phone me. It was quite a complicated business, because the phone call came on the day of my transfer from King's College Hospital to Kent and Canterbury Hospital. Both of them were on stand-by for them to phone, but in the end, the boys rang me on my mobile in the ambulance while I was between the two hospitals. I was asleep but Mum woke me up and I spoke to each of them. I don't think I made much sense because I was on so many drugs at the time.

We were sharing the ambulance with an elderly lady who had never heard of Blue. She thought Mum was a cruel mother for waking me up when I needed my sleep!

I felt very emotional today as we said goodbye to all the people who have looked after you. As the ambulancemen pushed you along the corridor, Chris gave you a cheery goodbye and tried to talk to me, but I couldn't see where I was going through the tears, let alone talk. You were tired and slept most of the way. My eyes kept welling up.

I felt secure at King's. I don't know what's going to happen at K & C, or how you might react to chemo.

At K & C you were put in an adolescent ward. The electric bed didn't work and not all your tablets are here yet. Still all you want to do is sleep. The journey has tired you out. I can have a separate room to sleep in but decided to sleep beside you tonight, as it's your first night in a strange place.

Thursday 6th February

They are still trying to get your tablets sorted, so you were in pain by the time they arrived. I thought I would order you some different food from a different menu, to see if that could entice you to eat, but it didn't. When one of the boys from Blazin' Squad phoned you this afternoon you went bright red and hid under the covers. Good to see some colour in your cheeks as you're very pale.

Your girls can walk from school to visit now, so they all arrived at 4 o'clock. Just as they had left, three more boys from Blazin' Squad phoned again.

Matron apologised for the initial hiccups. I also met Dr Martin, the consultant paediatrician. He talked about your care at K & C. Did I realise that you didn't have long to live and when would I tell you, as it might make it difficult for

74

*the nursing staff if you asked them any questions? These
are such difficult questions to deal with but I am adamant
that you will not be told until you are home.*

Friday 7th February

*We had a more relaxed day today as we start to establish
a routine. You had your first course of chemotherapy
tablets. They are quite big – you tell me it feels like
swallowing a grape. You have to take three of them, one
after the other.*

Saturday 8th February

*You were sick just after taking your tablets but we
couldn't give you any more, because we didn't know how
much you had absorbed.*

*Linda and Ian asked me to join them for a Chinese
meal tonight. It was very strange going outside for the
first time in two months and leaving you in hospital. I kept
thinking of you and wanted to leave the restaurant and
come back. There was a group of teenagers in the
restaurant celebrating a birthday, and I kept thinking that
you might not be here next year to celebrate yours. I*

wanted to tell Nanny and Linda that you didn't have long to live, and I know I should have done, but it just didn't feel like the right place to do it. I have to do it soon, but as it's your birthday tomorrow, I'll leave it until Monday.

Sunday 9th February

You are fourteen today and although I should be happy, I keep thinking this could be your last birthday. You opened all your birthday and Christmas presents. It was a lovely day with The Girls and family round you. Lee opened his presents a day early to be with you. I kept looking at everyone, laughing and smiling. I know I have to tell them all the terrible news tomorrow and it breaks my heart. You can't sit up as your back hurts and the chemo tablets are making you feel sick. You didn't even eat any birthday cake.

But Blazin' Squad remembered it was your birthday and phoned you again. It was such a nice thing to do and it made your day.

I have started to get a migraine, thinking about what I have to do tomorrow. I went home tonight for the first time. It was really strange. I felt lost without you being there, and kept thinking, this is what it would be like if you died.

My fourteenth birthday. To be honest, although the nurses were lovely and the other children came and sang 'Happy Birthday', I was miserable. I opened my birthday and Christmas presents. I'd been so ill that I hadn't bothered to open my Christmas presents before then. The Girls came to see me and brought me presents and a big card. They also brought my favourite cake, the chocolate caterpillar one. I cheered up a bit although I couldn't eat it.

There were between seventy and eighty get well and birthday cards. Everyone was being nice but I wanted them all to go away and stop fussing. It was all too much for one day.

When Strider from Blazin' Squad phoned to wish me a happy birthday I couldn't believe he had remembered, and it really cheered me up. Ant and Dec sent me a signed photo that wished me a 'Happy 15th Birthday' – which meant I could use it again the next year!

That same week I was asked if I would like to go to the Brits. I've always been into my music. I had just started my chemotherapy and couldn't even sit up in bed. I really wanted to go and remember pleading, but I was too ill. I can't believe I got an invite to the Brits and had to turn it down!

Monday 10th February

I was up early and back in hospital by your side at 7 a.m. Nanny is still at home looking after Lee. You missed me last night, so I told you any time you want me to stay, I will, and I won't go home again.

I asked Sue, the community nurse, to come in and help me tell Nanny and Linda this afternoon.

I realised at lunchtime I had forgotten to wish Lee a happy birthday. I feel terrible as my mind is on so many other things but I don't want him to feel left out.

Sue took us to a quiet room this afternoon, and I was glad she was there to explain everything. We all cried. We then tried to compose ourselves and came back to your bedside. It wasn't easy talking to you afterwards. I told Sue I will definitely tell you when you come home, which could be in a few weeks' time. I will tell Lee tomorrow as I don't want to do it today on his birthday. My migraine is thumping and I feel sick, but who am I to complain, compared to what you're going through?

Tuesday 11th February

I came home tonight to tell Lee. We both cried and hugged each other, and promised we would do all we

78

could to make your last few months as good as they can be.

Wednesday 12th February

I was crying as I drove to the hospital this morning at 7 a.m. It's hard to see people getting on with their lives, and children wearing your school uniform standing at bus stops.

But I have to snap out of this depression.

Nothing seems to be going right in this hospital. You need certain things that they haven't got here and Linda had to go to a clinic to get them. When there was another mix-up with your drugs, I asked Matron if I could have a meeting. The staff don't understand that they can't just come up to your bed and not say anything. I explained that this makes you nervous because you don't know who they are or what they are doing. She promised to pass on my concerns to the nurses.

Friday 14th February

I am not one to complain, it's not in my nature, but I felt so upset and annoyed about an incident that happened this morning, that I had to make an official complaint. I won't go into detail, but I felt that certain nurses weren't giving you the respect and dignity that you deserve. You are a fourteen-year-old girl who has just gone through a traumatic event leaving you blind and unable to move. You are totally dependent on those around you. Matron agreed with my complaint, and has now dealt with it.

Saturday 15th February

You were sick at 4 a.m. and were feeling sick from the chemotherapy for most of the day.

Things on the ward are better today but I stand by what I did. I feel I can never leave your bedside, which isn't the way it should be, but it will take me a while to regain my trust in the staff here.

I just want to take you home.

When King's College Hospital was planning to transfer me to Kent and Canterbury, they managed to organise a pass for Molly before they even got a bed for me. When nurses came to see me they would ask when Molly was coming in next. She was more famous than I was!

Sunday 16th February

Sue brought her dog, Miffy, in to see you. You liked her although you thought she was not as cuddly as Molly. I told Sue we'd like to go home as soon as possible and she agreed to start making the arrangements. You had several visitors today, luckily at different times of the day. You have taken anti-sickness tablets, which make you feel a bit better. You haven't eaten much again. You can't keep going on like this.

Monday 17th February

It's been the busiest day yet with visits from physiotherapists, a dietician, someone from the bed and equipment store, Jenny Seggie, Oena and two people from the catering department at the hospital. They all want to make your stay as pleasant as possible. The dietician suggested you drink milk if you can't eat, but it would have to be two pints of full-fat a day. The canteen have agreed they will cook anything you want if they can. We have ordered a wheelchair and other equipment that you'll need when you get home. The electric bed is also on order.

Tuesday 18th February

You were sick again last night. You won't eat as you think it will make you worse. You are struggling to swallow the tablets as they are so big, so we tried the chemo in liquid form. I have to make it up and keep it in a dark container in the fridge. If it is exposed to daylight it loses its strength. You gagged on it and couldn't finish the course, so we will go back to tablets tomorrow.

Nicola's mum, Robyn, brought The Girls to see you. I sat in the canteen telling her how you were deteriorating. Sue had arranged a meeting with The Girls and their parents at school to explain to them that if the chemo didn't work, then there was nothing else that could be done. I am relieved that it's now out in the open but hate deceiving you. You are so ill I don't think you could take the news. You might give up altogether if you think chemotherapy won't make any difference. I still believe in keeping it from you until you get home, which won't be long.

Around that time, I remember Mum bringing in photos she'd had developed. They were photos I had taken of The Girls at my sleepover just a few months earlier. I think it was the first time I realised just what being blind was going to feel like. I wanted to see the photos so much, but I couldn't so my friends described them to me. I felt left out because I couldn't see them, but I didn't let it show.

Wednesday 19th February

I had an appointment with Darren Hargraves at the Royal Marsden today, to discuss your treatment and care plan if the chemo doesn't work. It was a long and emotional meeting. I'm glad I took a small tape recorder with me, as I didn't think I would remember everything that was said. Everybody's main concern is that you don't know how ill you are and it's making me more and more upset. I know you best, and I know I'm right. I will not tell you until we get home. Darren doesn't think you are tolerating the chemo very well and said if you can't, then we will have to stop it and make the end of your life as comfortable as possible. I want to tell them that it's not like you to give up and they need to give you a chance. You are a fighter which you've already proved by what you've gone through. When I got back to you I told you some of the things he said, and you don't like the fact that people are giving up on you. We made a promise to each other that you will try harder to eat and do physio to get your strength back.

I really couldn't be bothered with physiotherapy. I just wanted to sleep. They used to come at 3 o'clock. I would check the time on my talking watch and when it said 2.55 p.m. I would pretend to sleep.

I thought one of the physios was much too bossy, but I know now that the bossy ones get good results. I moaned. It hurt – even sitting up in bed for a couple of seconds hurt.

I wish now I had done more physio, but at the time, I felt too weak, tired and sore.

But I remember the first day that a new physiotherapist got me out of bed. She said things like, 'Just try and do this – it doesn't matter if you can't.'

She gave me a choice. I sat up on the edge of the bed, slid on to a wooden board, then across to a wheelchair. I succeeded because I wasn't being bossed about and because I really wanted to do it. I was pushed around the ward in my wheelchair and went to show off to the doctors. Everyone was shocked to see me up. I went outside for the first time in three months. I remember the sun shining on my face. I spent about two hours in the chair. I remember feeling really happy.

Thursday 20th February

Your wheelchair arrived today. Your new physio, Clare, seems to have a way of explaining things in a way that you can visualise. Nobody could believe it when you spent about two hours in your wheelchair – for the past few weeks you have lain flat on your bed.

Sue says I need to get a carer for a few days a week to help me. I'm not too keen, but I have requested someone young and chatty, so they can keep you company. Sue has got three people in mind and will send them to meet you, so you can interview them and pick which one you get on with.

Friday 21st February

The Girls are going away with the school, so they came in to say goodbye as they won't see you for a while. You got out of bed into a comfy chair, which surprised them. When Linda came in this afternoon we took you outside in your chair and sat in the hospital garden for half an hour. You loved the fresh air and, although it is February, the sun was shining.

Saturday 22nd February

Lee is going to Scotland for a week to stay with Dad. He needs a break as there hasn't been a nice atmosphere around us lately. Everyone is just waiting for bad news.

Monday 24th February

I kept being told I needed a break so I reluctantly took the morning off. Nanny and the nurses looked after you until I came in at lunch-time. You didn't like it as no one knows your routine. You missed me and felt insecure. I wish I hadn't stayed away now.

Tuesday 25th February

You have been sick a lot today. You are very pale and have dark rings around your eyes. You haven't eaten for so long that I have stopped writing a food diary. You brought up the chemo tablets.

Wednesday 26th February

You have decided which of the carers you are going to choose. I had to meet Sue at home this afternoon, so we could go round the house with an occupational therapist to discuss what equipment you need. I don't know where I'm going to put a hoist, bath chair, wheelchair, commode, bedside table etc.

You really don't feel well today and just want to sleep.

Thursday 27th February

Had a meeting with the doctors as they think you are looking worse. They have changed your tablets and have given you some steroids. Sue has spoken to Linda, Nanny and me about how to look after you at home. She said it's getting urgent now to get you home as soon as possible as time could be running out. The electric bed is being delivered tomorrow, so Sue wants to get you home by the weekend.

Friday 28th February

I had to phone Lee in Scotland and explain to him that you were deteriorating and we are going to bring you home early. I don't want to send you to a hospice and Lee agrees. We will both look after you at home.

The van that the electric bed was in had an accident, so you can't go home. A new bed won't be delivered until next Friday. I don't want to be in hospital if anything happens to you. It's so impersonal.

Tuesday 4th March

You have been so ill over the past few days that Linda has carried your own bed downstairs into the living room so we can go home tomorrow. You won't be able to get upstairs now. You'll have to sleep in the living room. Now that you are going home I am feeling apprehensive but I know you have been so miserable in hospital and you are desperate to get home.

The ambulance arrived at 11.30 a.m. to take us home. I heard the ambulancemen ask a nurse if 'it' would happen on the way home. The nurse shushed them when I walked past. Again when we left this hospital I got the feeling that no one thought we would be back.

It is so quiet at home that you slept for three hours. You now have to get used to different sounds and smells, but at least you know where I am, as you know the layout of the house. At the hospital you couldn't hear anyone until they were right by your bed. I will sleep on the couch beside you until you feel comfortable to sleep downstairs alone. Molly is confused now that we're back. She doesn't know whose bed to sleep on. You can cuddle her anytime you want now and that comforts you.

Wednesday 5th March

Eighty-two days after going into hospital, I was home.

As the electric bed hadn't yet arrived, Linda had single-handedly carried my bed downstairs to the living-room.

When I came home, Kenzie from Blazin' Squad had phoned and left a message for me on the answer machine. It wasn't until halfway through that I realised who it was! Then the phone rang again and it was Kenzie to say he hadn't liked the message he'd left and that he was going to leave another one. He said hi to The Girls in the message as well. They almost screamed the house down when I played it to them. Molly was shaking in her bed! A few weeks later, Blazin' Squad sent me signed cards and CDs, five caps for me and The Girls, as well as belts, posters and a hoodie cardigan for me.

Thursday 6th March

The phone keeps ringing as everyone wants to know how you are. When the doorbell rings Molly barks and wakes you up. I've got to be strict now and have banned all phone calls between 2 p.m. and 5 p.m., so you can get some uninterrupted sleep. I have also made a 'do not disturb' sign for the front door. My main priority is to get your strength back to fight the disease and then hopefully you can tolerate the chemo properly. I have to think about including Lee as much as possible, as I don't want him to feel left out. I know it's not in his nature to feel like that, but I know we will never go back to the way we were. I just hope everyone will understand.

Friday 7th March

The electric bed came today. Molly doesn't like it when I put the sides up, because her legs are too short to jump over them on to the bed. So I've had to put a stool for Molly at the end of the bed.

I now have a book with columns for the time each drug is given, the name of the drug, the dose and a column for comments. Now I know at a glance that I have given you your tablets on time and if you're sick or feel pain I can tell the nurses when it happened.

Monday 10th March

This was the day that Mum told me that I hadn't got long to live. When two of my nurses explained that I would never walk or see again, I was devastated. Up until that point, I believed I would. Everything clicked into place the moment they asked what I wanted to do. I replied, 'Go shopping, but I'll go when I'm better and can walk.' It was then that they told me I had to do it now. That's when I thought, 'NO. I'm going to fight and I will prove everyone wrong.'

I did cry because I finally understood what people had been getting at. My body was giving up. Mum explained why she hadn't told me earlier. I believe she did the right thing.

Sue and Oena came to the house today to explain your prognosis to you. You were understandably upset and then angry that everybody thinks this is the end. You said

that you're not ready to die yet, and that you would prove
everybody wrong.

I'd like to think you could.

I looked at Sue and Oena for some reassurance, but
they could only smile sympathetically.

I'd take my chemotherapy three days a week for three
weeks, then have a week off, then start again. I felt ill
and was sick for a couple of days at the end of each
month's treatment.

Sometimes I was allowed a few weeks off between
each course. My hair would just start to grow, then fall
out again.

There were two kinds of chemo. One tablet was tiny
– smaller than a pea. The other was a capsule the size of
a giant grape. I took three of each tablet every night.
Fizzy drinks helped the big tablets go down more easily.

Mum kept a food diary when I got home. She wrote
down absolutely everything I ate. Even down to the
details like if I had ketchup on half a chip. She wrote
down how long I had been out of bed and what time I
had my tablets. I was on so many. I was taking them
every hour. At the most, when I was on my chemo, I
was taking twenty-seven tablets a day. That worked out
at about 190 tablets a week.

I had funny food patterns. For example, I had a thing

about pork scratchings and I could eat two or three bags a day. I cleared out the local suppliers. I had family and friends bringing me about five bags at a time! And then after about two months I went off them. The new craving was bacon sandwiches. For the next two months I had one every morning and sometimes one for lunch. Lee made the best bacon sandwiches. I went off them too, and then on to smoky bacon crisps – I think I must have had a thing for pigs!

It took a long time for me to start eating properly because my stomach had shrunk.

Molly was on my lap constantly – she, Mum and The Girls helped get me through that time. I took my last chemo tablets on Wednesday 18th February 2004, Nicola's birthday. And I've gone from strength to strength ever since.

You know everyone has a song? Mine is 'Beautiful' by Christina Aguilera. Not because I'm being bigheaded, but when I was in hospital – I'd just had the stroke, my face was twisted with Bell's palsy, I had tubes in my arms and one through my nose to feed me, scratches on my face and basically felt awful – I kept hearing that song on the radio. It might sound cheesy, but it made me feel better, and not the freak I sometimes felt I was.

Lee bought me the single when it was released.

There's No Place Like Home

Baldilocks

When I was at school, I wrote a story about Baldilocks and the Three Hairs. I didn't know then that I would become Baldilocks myself . . .

I lost my hair at the end of February 2003. I remember Mum saying to me a couple of days before, 'You're lucky, your hair hasn't fallen out,' but then it did. I told her that she had jinxed me.

I used to pull it out and put it in the sick bucket beside the bed. The bucket was clean but my hair wasn't. I couldn't help myself! Because I couldn't see it, I'd rub it on my chin first to see how much came out. All of my hair fell out except three determined hairs that remained throughout the nine months of chemotherapy. I couldn't get rid of them. It was my hair after all.

Although it was upsetting to lose my hair, I think I was extremely lucky as it was the only real side effect of the chemotherapy. I lost the hair on my legs, which saved me having to wax them! But I kept my eyebrows and eyelashes. (By this I mean they didn't fall out, and not that I kept them in a sick bucket too!)

We sent a sample of my hair to a company that made wigs. Mum described the wigs in their catalogues to me – they came in all kinds of styles, even party wigs. The wig they sent me was layered to my shoulders. Although they had made the wig the same colour as the sample of hair we'd sent, it looked odd because my face was so pale. I used to wear hats so that it looked more like my own hair but it was hot and itchy. I also had a blue bandana with hundreds of plaits attached along the bottom of it which was lovely and soft against my baldness. The plaits had copper highlights in them so they looked better against my pale skin. I wore the bandana most of the time. I wore different hats with it to make it look a bit different. I had about twenty hats, almost all of them – unsurprisingly – pink!

In the summer it was good to be bald because my head didn't get hot. It was cold in the winter though. I didn't have to worry about washing my hair every day but I had to wash my head occasionally! People would tell me that I had a nicely-shaped head, which made me laugh. 'It's just a head,' I thought, 'what's so nice about it?' I always wore my wig outside but in the house I held my hairless head high. I kept my wig on a polystyrene head. Visitors would do a double-take. Someone waved at it once until they saw the real me sitting on the couch. Some people who saw me bald don't visit me any more. I regret that a little bit. Only people who genuinely cared should have been able to see me with no hair.

No more Baldilocks. It was such a great feeling when my hair started growing back. I got Mum to measure it with a ruler and each time it was a little bit longer. For Rachel's birthday, I gave myself a Mohican style and put pink glitter along the top.

Even now I still run my hands through my hair to check that it isn't coming out. This is the only lasting side effect. I realise that future treatment may mean that I lose it again, but now I know that it will probably grow back.

Losing my hair made me realise it's only hair at the end of the day. It's not your whole life – although it could end up costing you your life, if you're vain enough to refuse chemotherapy because of it. I'd rather be alive and bald than dead and hairy – your hair's no good when you're dead! In fact, *Alive and Bald or Dead and Hairy* was going to be the title of this book at one stage.

Needles . . .

My biggest fear is needles. I'm petrified of them. I feel really panicky just thinking about them.

The fear begins to build from the moment – about an hour before the cannula is due – the nurse applies the numbing cream, making my way to the ward, waiting for the doctor, the sound of the trolley coming down the corridor, the opening of packets, the clicking of the bits connecting, the taking off of the sticky plaster with the cream, the wiping the cream off, the smell of the wipe to clean my hand, the band put round the top of my arm, the pillow put under my hand, the tapping of my hand for the vein to pop up, the doctor and nurses asking questions about the weather or something else to take my mind off it, putting my hand in a fist, the doctor taking my hand, feeling they think I'm a baby and should grow up, me saying don't tell me when it's happening, knowing full well when it is happening because there is always a wait, and then – finally – the needle is pushed in and wiggled about to get it in the right position. And that's if it's worked the first time.

Sometimes I've needed it done three or four times to get it in the right place. I have two scars on my wrist where a needle went in and was bandaged up not realising that it had worked its way through another part of the skin on my wrist. I don't worry about any of my treatment or my results. But I do worry about needles. Although I've noticed that every time I get a needle stuck in me, I become that little bit stronger.

Because I felt quite well during the chemotherapy, I managed to avoid frequent blood tests. Once, the nurse used a little needle that shot in and out of my finger, catching the drops of blood in a pot. I much prefer this method to a normal blood test. I have to put my hand in hot water, wrap it in a hot flannel, then put it in a poly bag to keep it warm until my thumb is pricked. The test always came back fine, even if my blood count was low – that was to be expected.

Never Give Up!

I genuinely believed that I would – eventually – get back to normal, and for me, normal meant walking, seeing and shopping. I've always loved shopping. So when I was asked in hospital what I most wanted to do, that was what I said.

But of course, it wasn't that simple. Even by the end of March 2003 I found it hard to spend a long time in my wheelchair and got backache, so the community nurse – with the help of Dave Lee's Happy Holidays Charity – arranged for me to go to the Bluewater Shopping Centre in a white stretch limo.

We needed an occupational therapist to get me into the limo. I had never moved from my chair into a car before. I sat on a kind of wooden boomerang thing that helped slide me on to the seat. The limo was parked outside our house and I felt a bit self-conscious, excited but anxious at the same time.

I took Mum, Nicola, Rachel, Kerry and Charlotte with me. Lee sat in the front with the driver, Tim. It was a left-hand-drive limo, so it looked as if Lee was our driver. I lay along the middle seat, with Mum and Nicola at the seats across my feet and Kerry, Rachel and Charlotte on the seats by my head. This was the first time in over three months that I had dressed properly. I wore a pink polo neck that Mum had bought for me for Christmas and a pair of pale jeans that didn't fit any more. You could probably have fitted two of me in them. But it felt good to get dressed, as if I was making real progress.

The Girls screamed when they saw the stretch limo. I hadn't told them how we were travelling. Tim was great – even though I called him Dim Tim from time to time! He pushed me around the centre and even went into the Disney shop to get me some posters.

The shopping trip was a learning experience for us all. I had everything described to me and had to feel everything too. I bought lots of things, including my first hat. It was white with FCUK in pink across the front. I remember wondering if people were staring at me but generally I didn't care. It was just great to be there, shopping with my friends, after everything that had happened. Mum bought party hats for the journey home – but she also brought some alcopops, so I forgave her for the hats. I drank mine lying down with a straw. I remember crying, though, because I couldn't drink properly. The day was filled with so many emotions.

Challenges and Charities

While I was in hospital Dad gave me a huge bear. It filled an armchair and was too big to stay in the house. I donated it to my school so that they could raffle it. I was desperate to be involved so Rachel brought all the money they had raised home and we spent four hours counting it, and I threw all the notes in the air afterwards – I loved doing that! The money was sent to CLIC – Cancer and Leukaemia In Children.

Mr Gugenheim, one of Nicole's teachers at Barton Court Grammar School, recalls Nicole's growing involvement with various charities.

Nicole asked me not to mention her situation to the year group at assemblies because she was adamant that she did not want people to sympathise. We did organise a raffle for a huge teddy bear to raise funds for CLIC. That led me to mention Nicole, but never because we thought she was dying. We raised nearly £500 as I recall.

CLIC, Demelza House and Riding for the Disabled became Nicole's rocks and helped her in so many ways. In typical Nicole style, she has spent most of her time trying to repay their help in any way she can, and I believe that she has done that extraordinarily successfully.

Jeffrey

Because I wasn't well enough to go back to school, other arrangements had to be made, and in June 2003 Evelyn came to see me. It was Evelyn who introduced me to Braille. It wasn't always easy and I was often frustrated because after the stroke I could only use two fingers on my right hand so I was very slow. But gradually I improved, and I began to learn Braille numbers too.

I also started getting talking books and my favourite magazines on tape. They still come once a week through the post. I keep in touch with all the soap gossip and celebrity news. I love my gossip!

Evelyn has been a brilliant friend to me, and has helped me a lot over the years.

Evelyn specialises in teaching children with visual impairments.

I had been told that Nicole was totally blind, had terminal cancer and that her life expectancy was very short. I knew this was going to be a very different assignment to my usual workload and I wasn't sure what to expect or whether or not I would have anything to offer. With some apprehension I made my first visit.

At the time Nicole was fourteen years old. She had come home from hospital, as there was nothing further the medical profession could do except to try chemotherapy to treat the inoperable tumours on her spine. On arriving I was warmly greeted by Molly, Nicole's dog, and told by Jackie, Nicole's mother, that Nicole and Molly were as one. Nicole was sitting in an armchair, pale, thin and with no hair. A few metres away was a hospital bed which had been put in the sitting-room as Nicole could no longer use the stairs to get to her own room. As I sat down the apprehension was overwhelming. What could I possibly do for this young girl?

My eye caught sight of a photograph, above the bed, of Nicole and her brother, taken before this illness had taken such a hold of her. The photograph didn't give me the reassurance that I needed but it rather made me feel more unsettled, seeing Nicole there in the picture as a once happy and healthy young person. I can't quite remember how the conversation started but I began to be aware of someone sitting in front of me talking non-stop about some of the things that mattered to her – animals, friends and the colour pink. She seemed so normal and intelligent and I gradually felt myself relaxing. I began to talk about Braille. I could see that she seemed interested, and curious as to how she would manage the challenge when she had so little mobility in her right hand. We agreed we would give it a try and I promised that I would put any Braille I brought along on to pink card. I wasn't totally convinced that Braille was going to be the answer but it would be something on which to focus, a challenge, and possibly give her some independence, even if it was for only a very short time.

Over the next few months we persevered with the Braille. During that time I got to know Nicole better and looked forward to working with her. She had a wonderful sense of humour and was fun to be with. Some Braille sessions had to be curtailed, though, as Nicole could tire or her back would begin to get uncomfortable with sitting. She often needed to rest after a session and sleep.

Then gradually Nicole appeared to be getting stronger. It was difficult to ask either her or her mother, at that time, what the prognosis was, and whether she was going to beat this cancer. During that period I was also reassessing the value of Braille to Nicole. Nicole's need for independence was moving faster than Braille was offering. It isn't easy to learn Braille when coming to it at a later age, and having very limited mobility in her right hand didn't help either. So I began thinking about what else could possibly help her. I decided to request, from *the Local Education Authority, a laptop computer with speech software. I knew I had to teach her to touch-type before she could make any real use of the computer but I thought that it could give her another kind of independence and possibly one further-reaching than Braille. It was worth a try. Two years on, she has now written well over 100,000 words on her laptop, uses email proficiently, and has been able to share her story in print and online with very many people.*

I call the voice on my laptop 'Jeffrey'. He has an American accent which was annoying at first but I'm used to him now. I got used to the keyboard by learning to touch-type, and to give myself some extra practice, I started to write my autobiography. I never knew what to write, so I decided to just note down what I had done each day, and began to enjoy it. I then thought I'd write about what had happened to me during the last four years, and it developed into a book from there. I also have a secret diary which is where I let off steam – even Mum has never read it . . .

Jeffrey is also on my mobile phone. When I press a key, it reads everything aloud to me and when my friends send text messages the phone reads them aloud too.

Scotland, Sox and Silver Lining

Out and about

In September 2003, I flew to Scotland with Mum and Lee. It was the first time that I had travelled on a plane as a disabled person.

At the airport, before we even got on the plane, I had a bit of a tantrum. We had been told we would be the first people on the plane with another disabled lady. I was pleased because it meant no one would be staring at me. We went to the front of the queue but the airport staff started letting everyone else on first. They told us we would be the last to board. I started crying, shouting and swearing while this nice old lady, the other disabled person, sat there without making a fuss. I was a bit emotional in those days! On the runway I was put on a chair with wheels. Two men lifted me up the stairs on to the plane and, of course, everyone looked out of the window to see what was going on.

When we arrived at Lesley's house, the community

nurses had organised an electric bed and ramps to help me in and out of the house. It was a great week. I was still taking my chemo tablets, but I didn't feel ill. Needless to say, I didn't come back from Scotland with a tan!

Since October 2003, I have been learning to ride with the Riding for the Disabled Association (RDA), and the following April, I won the cup for being the Most Improved Rider. It was a huge cup, presented to me at a barbeque at the stables, and it sat on our TV for a year, before I had to give it back.

Horse-riding has strengthened my legs, helping me reach my goal to walk.

My RDA horse, Sox, is 15.3 hands high – she's quite a tall horse. She stands beside the lift which raises me to the correct height. I stand up and a helper lifts my leg over the saddle so that I can sit down and wiggle myself into position. Jane, Sox's owner, holds a leader rope and two helpers walk on either side in case I fall off. I never feel scared riding Sox. I can't see how high I am when I'm sitting on her, so I don't feel nervous.

When I went back to see Chris Chandler in January 2004 to show off how well I was doing, I asked him if I could do a bungee jump for charity – he didn't really have an answer, but said that it was up to me. I haven't decided to do it yet, but there's still time . . . !

Family, friends and fun

My family is very important to me – especially Mum and Lee. One night in April 2004 Lee rang Mum. It was about 11 p.m. I was in bed downstairs and I could hear Mum upstairs on the phone. I knew something was wrong. She was saying, 'Lee, are you all right?' I thought he had been stabbed or something so I was quite relieved when Mum came downstairs and told me he had only been hit by a bus!

Mum went to pick him up from Canterbury, fifteen minutes away.

Lee had been out with his mates and they went to catch the last bus home. Lee attempted to flag the bus down when he saw it about to leave the station, but realised it wasn't going to stop and turned to walk away. The bus hit him in the back, knocking him to the ground. I don't think the driver could have seen Lee, despite the fact that he was wearing a brand new (expensive) white jacket! As he fell the pocket was ripped off and he landed on an oily tyre mark which left a print making it look as if he had been run over. Lee was really winded. He said he wanted to cry but (I quote) 'There was a load of fit birds around, so I couldn't!'

It was 2 a.m. when he got back and we sat up and

had a cup of tea. Lee was acting really weird. He was talking a lot and really fast. I think it was the shock. Mum described his back to me. It was cut from the top of his spine to the top of his butt cheeks, red-raw and with the skin peeling off. He took painkillers and went to bed. The next day Mum took Lee to hospital. It took a while for his back to heal and he still gets backache now and again. We laugh about it. It's something to put on your grave – *Hit by a Bus!* It's strange, but I almost enjoyed all the fuss because Lee got the attention for a while. People were asking about him and not me for a change.

In October we moved into our new home. As we had moved to a bungalow I got my own room back. It was a bit weird having my own room again because in the last house I had been sleeping in the living-room for nearly two years. It was too difficult for me to get upstairs.

My room has been organised so that everything is in a place where I know that I can reach the things I need. Mum painted my bedroom furniture pink, the colour of Piglet. I've got my pink rug on the floor and lots of pink boxes on the side. Everything I have is pink.

To celebrate my fifteenth birthday we had a big family meal at a Beefeater restaurant, partly because it was close by and partly because I knew I could order garlic bread and chips! I am still a very fussy eater. The next day was Lee's eighteenth birthday. We went to the Bluewater Shopping Centre again in a limo – I knew that I would enjoy it properly this time. My friend did my make-up. I can still remember what I was wearing – turned up jeans with beige suede boots, a long pink suede jacket with pink fur round it, my wig with the plaits and my pink Beatle cap. The Girls said that I looked like a superstar!

I can't remember what I bought that time, but we had a really fun day, singing and eating chocolates in the limo on the way home.

To help me have more confidence I like to look as good as I possibly can. I don't like a lot of make-up, but it's essential to have some! I can tell the different bottles and boxes apart by their smell, feel and shape. My technique for putting mascara on involves measuring the distance between the wand and my eyes with my fingers, then holding my hand against my nose so that the brush is at just the right angle for me to blink rapidly, coating my eyelashes in the mascara.

I choose which perfume I'm going to wear, feel where the nozzle is, place it against my wrist and then pull back a few centimetres so that I know I'm aiming for the right place. Then, squirt! I always close my eyes too, just in case it goes wrong!

Doctors and designing

As well as my riding lessons, I began to get involved in fundraising. The Silver Lining Appeal raises funds to update equipment in King's College Hospital where I'd been treated, and I was invited to Dulwich as an ambassador for the launch night in May 2004, where I was presented with a special badge – of a rainbow coming out of a cloud. Linda Barker, the designer, was amongst the celebrities at the event.

At the Silver Lining Appeal Christmas party in 2004 I met Anthony Costa from Blue. Just before the end of the party Mum took me out into the corridor where I was told someone wanted to meet me. I thought it was going to be Chris Chandler, so I was totally surprised when I then heard, 'Hi, it's Anthony from Blue.' I was so shocked that I couldn't speak – and it takes a lot to shut me up! I was really paranoid that he was looking at my nose, because I'd had it pierced and it had got infected two days earlier, and I had to take the stud out. I had a bit of a scab on the side of my nose, and he was standing that side of me! He was really nice, and I couldn't stop smiling afterwards.

Demelza House is one of my favourite places. It's a house specially adapted for people with disabilities, and although I had been for a day visit, I went for

At age 10, sporty and active, before Nicole's illness

Age 11, 2000 – with the hated tumour.

December 2000, after her first operation and radiotherapy, Nicole presenting a cheque to the Sargeant Cancer Care charity.

Age 14, March 2003 – Nicole and The Girls get ready for their Bluewater shopping trip.

Age 16, 2005 – Nicole stands and takes her first steps after an operation to flatten her feet.

(From left to right: Lesley, Jackie, Nicole and Gloria)

Age 16, 2005 – Nicole rides Sox with the Riding for the Disabled Association.

Age 18, 2007 – Nicole and Daizy.

June 2007 – Mum, Jackie, helps Nicole sign her book contract.

my first weekend in July 2004. I was a bit nervous about staying overnight for the first time but the carers and other children were so friendly that I soon relaxed. I had a carer with me all the time. One of the highlights of my stay was 'meeting' a tortoise. She was blind so I had to hand-feed her. On her tummy she was smooth and wrinkly. She felt quite weird! I've loved tortoises ever since.

Mum stayed too as I didn't want to be left completely on my own but she let the carers look after me. I had a facial, my make-up done and my eyebrows waxed. I had my hair trimmed for the first time in two years. I did ask Linda, the carer, if she was licensed to be a hairdresser! I didn't have a lot of hair at the time and I thought if it was cut it might ruin what had already grown. She was under strict instructions just to even it up where it had grown back, after chemo, at different stages. She blow-dried it and put wax in it, and I felt great!

It gave me a bit of independence and confidence to be away from Mum. I was just so used to her being there for me that I didn't think I could cope without her, but I did! I felt a bit rude asking people for help – getting me a drink or pushing me back to my room – but they didn't mind.

The Demelza House Children's Hospice was opened in 1998. It was designed to feel like a home-from-home, with its very own dog, Coco, a chocolate Labrador. It's not like a hospital at all – there is a Jacuzzi, a massage room, an art and music room and a sensory room which includes a warm water bed, water tubes, beanbags and relaxing music, padded flooring and fibre optics. On my first visit I fed the goats and a sheep, and had a massage, but spent the majority of the time in the art room making presents. I have become more involved with Demelza House over the years. The aim of the hospice is to add life to days when days cannot be added to life.

I was asked if I would like to design an adolescent room. We called the room TIZ (short for The Inclusion Zone) and it is for teenagers over the age of fifteen. I went to meetings every couple of months with another girl called Shahira, and two boys, Chris and Wesley. We said what we wanted in the room, the colours etc. It took about eighteen months to build and design. The room has comfy leather sofas, plasma screen TV, brilliant sound system, lots of CDs and DVDs, a kitchen with the latest gadgets, giant beanbags and lots more. We came up with the idea of everyone designing a jigsaw piece with their favourite things on it, so that they can all be slotted together and put on the wall. In 2005 we won a Philip Lawrence Award for our work on The Inclusion Zone.

I have organised a few fundraising events for Demelza House. At one of my coffee mornings, at St Nicholas' School, I raised nearly £500. There were all kinds of stalls – crafts, cakes, tea, a tombola, bring-and-buy. And I also sold copies of a book of poems I'd written, which people asked me to sign! Over 120 people came to support me.

In July 2004 I was asked if I would be a guinea pig for student doctors to try and diagnose what is wrong with me. I am a difficult case and the student doctors couldn't work out what was wrong with me.

They felt my legs and tested my strength. I knew from previous check-ups that for part of that routine I needed to interlock my hands and pull. When the first student said, 'Can you do this?', demonstrating by using his own hands, I knew what he meant and did it. But he hadn't realised that I'm blind – he was supposed to have worked that out. After he left the room I was told not to help the next student. When he asked me to do the same thing, I had to say, 'Do what?' He demonstrated it again and when I didn't respond he realised that I couldn't see, so he put my hands together for me. I don't think any of the students guessed all my problems – and I haven't been asked back to do it again. Maybe I'm just too complicated a case!

More Ups Than Downs

December 2004

I got a special Advent calendar for 2004. It was a 3-D tree made out of cardboard with little drawers with chocolates in. Evelyn bought it for me and taught me Braille numbers. She then stuck Braille numbers on the drawers. They weren't in order so I couldn't cheat!

I had my second fundraising coffee morning, at my friend Diana's house, in December 2004. I had been very busy and made things to sell such as home-made cards and decorations. I made them in my art lesson at school. I made them by feeling everything and I said exactly where I wanted things stuck. We had a raffle, a bring-and-buy table, tea and cakes. It went really well. I raised £471.30 for Demelza House, which I was really pleased with.

I was also in *Best* magazine in December 2004. An agency had contacted me to see if I would tell my story. I had a photo-shoot in October for it, which was quite strange because the photographer brought a load of

Christmas decorations with him, as the story was being published at Christmas. I was excited about being in the magazine, but I cringed when it came out. They had the main facts but they had changed the way I said it and so it sounded really cheesy! The headline was 'Santa was the last person I saw before I went blind' – although that was what happened, I didn't want it to sound miserable. I wanted the article to sound positive and happy because that is how I feel. People who know me know that's not the way I talk. Overall though, I was happy with the article and hopefully people who read it will have thought that it was a nice story.

The same month I met Steve from the Kent Association for the Blind. He started to teach me to use JAWS (a screen reader) more efficiently. He has a visual impairment himself. Steve was learning things along with me. He was used to his own keyboard and had to work out things for me as the layout on my laptop was slightly different. Soon I had worked out how to send, receive and reply to emails. It made me more independent because before, Mum used to have to read them out to me. He also taught me shortcuts on the keyboard and how to use the Internet.

Lessons from the KAB also helped me with writing my book. Evelyn would take my laptop home with her to review sections of it and see if there were any obvious mistakes. She made a point about me not mentioning that I am blind. I had never thought of that before then. It's not that I hide the fact that I can't see, I just don't think like that. A lot of things in my book that I have described have been described to me in the first place, so I find it easy to form a picture in my head. I feel as though I am actually seeing it. I don't feel blind although that might sound stupid. I have just got used to it. I don't wake up and think, 'Oh, I'm blind.' It has never really bothered me and it doesn't stop me doing much, so sometimes I forget! Because my eyes still move in the same way that a sighted person's eyes move, many people don't even realise that I'm blind.

I loved shopping for Christmas presents that year with my carer Nikki. I wanted to wrap them myself. I had to keep hiding the presents under my duvet because most of them were for Mum. Mum kept coming into my room to make sure I was putting the paper the right way up. I only wrapped one inside out! I had the Sellotape on one of those dispensers, so it was easy for me to just pull a piece off. That then ran out and I had to use the normal Sellotape on a roll. I kept losing the end of it. It's hard enough trying to find it anyway, but being blind just makes it so much harder. I started getting annoyed with it. All the paper had jaggy edges because I couldn't cut it properly. It was fine wrapping square presents, but funny shapes like stars just aren't meant to be wrapped!

Since I came out of hospital, it's become a tradition for The Girls to come to my house to give each other our presents. They always come a few days before Christmas, and the room is full of paper and presents afterwards. Nikki painted my nails with a Christmas theme. I had a Santa with googly eyes and holly and mistletoe, reindeers and snowmen.

On Christmas Eve I was really excited, but the night before I was ill. I had really bad pains in my stomach. It felt like being stabbed repeatedly. I had backache and all my joints ached. I had a temperature and a headache as well. I was in so much pain. It turned out that I had a urine infection, so I was put on antibiotics. I was adamant I wasn't going to spend another Christmas in hospital, but part of me thought I might have to.

It was the year of the tsunami. I remember we had just arrived at Linda's when she got a call from her friend to see if she had heard the news about the earthquake and tidal waves in South East Asia. All day the number of people who had died was rising. I kept hearing the news about the countries that were affected by the flooding. Thousands died. It was hard to imagine that amount of people. I would forget about it until I listened to the news again. Some people will never forget and especially if they knew someone who had died. Linda's friend lost her two young sons and her fiancé.

2005

In January I had my first English lesson with Hilary. I started having English lessons to help me to write my book. The first time we met we didn't do much work. We just chatted and wrote about pink things. That week Lee had to take me to school to have my art lesson with my teacher, Yvonne, as Mum had been ill for nearly a week. She had a really bad migraine. It was the first time I had been in the car with Lee since he'd passed his test in September 2004. It was a really different experience to Mum's driving!

I started coming home from school on the minibus three days a week. Mum was more nervous than I was! Soon I was at school every day. Before Christmas I was only doing three days a week and the other two days used to be my shopping and chilling out days. I got to pick the subjects I wanted to do, which were art, cooking, music and physiotherapy. I started to learn the guitar, but I was told that my nails were too long and I had to cut them. The nails won, so then I moved on to the keyboard but that didn't last long either.

I had a urine infection on my sixteenth birthday, so wasn't feeling too well. Family had been round in the morning and I'd opened presents. I went to lie down for a bit in the afternoon because I was tired, and then Mum asked if I wanted to walk back to the living-room. I said I couldn't be bothered, but would walk from halfway up the corridor. Mum pushed me in my chair to the living-room door, and I stood up with my walking frame. I walked a few steps but got really frustrated with my foot. The ligament was so tight at the back – it had shortened from spending a lot of time in bed – that I was walking like I had a high heel on. I was also walking on the side of my foot. I got so annoyed that I shouted, 'This foot is f**king spasticated. It's not f**king working!' Just then my three teachers from school started quietly and nervously singing 'Happy Birthday'. I didn't know they were coming, so it was a bit of a surprise. I was supposed to have been at school that afternoon, but hadn't gone because I was ill. Lee had let them in and told them to be quiet, so I hadn't heard them. It might have been funny if they'd laughed. Not so sweet sixteen! I enjoyed that birthday but wasn't looking forward to the next one when I would be seventeen. I knew all my friends would be getting cars and having driving lessons but I would never be able to drive. I thought about it in a positive way though – I would be chauffeured around instead.

I was invited to the Dorchester Hotel for a Chocolate Ball in March. It was in aid of CLIC (Cancer and Leukaemia in Children) and Sargent Cancer Care. They were amalgamating to become one charity – CLIC Sargent. I was really looking forward to it, especially once I started to find out more about it. There was going to be a giant chocolate Jenga, a chocolate fountain, celebrities and music. As the event was at the Dorchester Hotel, I was going to have to dress posh! I bought my outfit the week before – all colour co-ordinated and very sparkly. We had been given four tickets so I was taking Mum, Lee and a friend. Then a few days before the event, I got another urine infection. I think I had a bit of a chest infection too. I started a course of antibiotics but they hadn't helped by the time the day of the ball arrived. I hadn't been out of bed for days, and just hours before it was to start I had no choice but to cancel. I've never been so disappointed. I also felt that I'd let everyone down because they had all been looking forward to it. Being a chocoholic it would have been Mum's ideal party. It was such a waste of the tickets – but the organisers sent me a goody bag which cheered me up.

I seemed to be ill for all of March. I couldn't get rid of the urine infections, so I was feeling quite fed up. Everything came to a head when my carer, Nikki, was doing my nails. She asked if I was OK, and I just burst out crying. I didn't really know what was wrong. I think everything from the previous two years had just hit me. I was used to being so positive and bubbly, that I didn't quite know what was wrong. It wasn't a specific thing. I hadn't seen my friends for over a month because there had been bad snow, and I was waiting to see a specialist about fixing my foot, but there was a long waiting list. I was down for a couple of days, but soon felt better. I think I just needed to let it all out.

By April I was feeling better – and the results of that month's scans showed that the shadows on my spine were staying stable. Nikki looked after me for a couple of days each week for over a year and we had become good friends. She took me out shopping quite a lot and she helped me organise surprises for Mum. It was a shock when she told me she was leaving because I no longer needed palliative care. I asked what she meant and she carefully tried to explain. I quickly understood what she was trying to say, so I said, 'You mean caring for the dying?' I hadn't realised it was the reason she had been looking after me. I was glad I didn't know what it was until after I had been taken off it.

In April the Wish Foundation arranged for Mum,

Lee and me to go to Tenerife for a week, and to visit Loro Park where I could swim with dolphins. I had picked swimming with dolphins as my wish because I knew I could get in the water with them and feel them. This was the first time that I had been abroad. We stayed in a lovely hotel in Port de la Cruz.

The holiday started off quite embarrassingly. We had just arrived at our hotel room. I was having a lie-down because my back hurt, and Mum and Lee went to the restaurant to get some food. We had called reception when we arrived to say that the fridge in our room wasn't working. While Mum and Lee were away a man came to fix it. He came in the room and said, 'Hola.' I hadn't yet worked out the layout of the room in my head, and so I waved in front of me and said, 'Hola,' to where I thought he was standing. It wasn't until Mum came back that she said that I'd waved at the wall, and he had been standing behind me!

The wheel on my wheelchair nearly fell off while we were there. I think it got damaged on the plane on the way out. The wheel was splaying out, and we really thought it was going to fall off. Lee had to push me about, like a wheelbarrow, for a few days. We then hired another wheelchair, but that was just as bad.

On the sixth day we were shown around Loro Park, and then we watched the dolphin show. Everyone left the arena after the show, and then it was time for my wish. I was told I would wear a wetsuit but decided it would be too difficult to get into one. Luckily I had put on my hotpants under my skirt because I ended up going in the water in just my shorts and T-shirt. The five Spanish guys that worked with the dolphins lifted me out of my chair and put me on the edge of the platform with my feet dangling in the water. Only one of the men could speak English so he sat next to me and had his arm around me the whole time. He explained everything and let me feel the different parts of one of the dolphins. I felt in its mouth, and its nose which is shorter than I thought. I tried to kiss it but it didn't want me to so it jumped up and poked me in the eye! He sent that one away and another dolphin swam over. This one was called Taina. She was the baby who was eleven years old. She came and rested her head on my lap and I stroked her. She let me kiss her on the nose a few times. She smelt of fish! Lovely!

Lee filmed me with them while they were doing their tricks. Their fins and tails were very hard but their bodies were warm and soft. Their skin also felt silky and a little bit rubbery. The warm water just fell off their backs. At the end all seven dolphins came and swam round my feet. Then the trainers wagged their fingers and the dolphins sang to me – it was ear-piercingly loud!

I waved goodbye and they all swam on their backs and flapped their tails to say 'bye'. It was a great holiday.

In May I did a two-hour sponsored silence to raise money for Dave Lee's Happy Holidays, who send poorly children on holiday, and who paid for my limo trips to Bluewater. I had it at my friend Gilly's house. Her children and their friends took part too, and there were around twelve of us. We were silent for an hour, then had a ten-minute break, then did the second hour. All the children had games and pens and paper to write notes to each other, and I listened to a tape. We raised around £750.

I baked cakes at school for the sponsored silence. They were fairy cakes. Half of them had baby pink icing with white chocolate drops on top and the others had fuchsia pink icing with little heart, star and flower-shaped icing bits. They were very girlie and they tasted good too!

It was in the summer that I decided that I want to be a designer and design clothes for wheelchair users. I get annoyed with my trousers being too short when I sit down. They are a normal length when I stand but get shorter when I am sitting (which is all the time) and it doesn't help that I have legs as long as a giraffe's!

One of my first days out on my own with my friends ended up being quite eventful! I was in Canterbury with

Kerry, Charlotte, Rachel and Nicola, and we had nearly finished shopping. Mum was in town too, and told me to ring her when I wanted picking up. One of The Girls was pushing me when we hit a grate sticking up in the street. I had pink silk covering my chair at the time, so I just slid off. I put my hands out to break my fall, then rolled over and just sat. We didn't quite know what to do, so The Girls sat on the ground with me so I didn't look too weird. There were lots of people around who saw what happened, but they didn't bother to help. I then called Mum and said, 'Can you come and pick me up, please?' She replied, 'Are you ready then?' and I said, 'No, pick me up off the floor!' I was fine apart from some cuts on my hands, and I was shaking, but that was with shock. I actually found it quite funny! The strange thing was that I had been a bit nervous about going out shopping, but while I was sitting on the ground I just thought, 'I don't care!' I'd arranged to go out that day to help boost my confidence. I'd never felt confident going out somewhere public in the school holidays in case I met someone I knew. I'd normally stay in and hibernate! That day helped – and I hold on now when I'm on bumpy streets! I had to fall out of my chair one day, I just didn't expect to be in the middle of Canterbury when I did it!

Rosettes and trophies

On 7th June I took part in my first competition at Hickstead. I had been practising my routine for months, and was a little bit nervous about it. I felt really posh because I had to wear a smart jacket, silky hat, frilly shirt and a hairnet! (I wasn't too impressed with that bit.) They made Sox look really pretty. She had her mane tied in little knots, had her hoofs painted shiny black, conditioner in her tail to make it shine, and patterns brushed into her coat at the back. I did my routine and was quite happy with it apart from at the end. I slightly pulled the reins too much one way, so instead of bowing forward to the judges, I bowed more to the fence! I wasn't happy with what I did and wanted to do it again. There were a few hours before the results, but I came seventh out of twenty-three. The annoying thing was that the rosettes only went up to sixth place! I hadn't got any extra marks for being blind, so I was quite pleased with my result in the end.

On 9th June I won two Try Angle Awards. They are awards for 11–18-year-olds in Kent for special achievements. I won the enterprise category for my fundraising, and the Lord Mayor's Triumph Over Adversity award. It was the first year anyone had won two, so I was really pleased with that. We went to a ceremony where everyone was presented with their awards. I got two engraved Perspex triangle-shaped trophies, and two framed certificates. There were around nine different categories, with three winners in each. There was an overall winner for each category too, which was announced on the night, so no one knew who had won. I won both my categories, which was a big shock, and I got two more framed certificates.

After the awards I started appearing in my local paper. They asked to write a story about me, which then turned into a middle-page double spread. When I was emailing someone from the paper about something they had wanted to know, I asked if there was any chance of a regular column – if you don't ask, you don't get! I didn't get an answer, but it was worth a try!

Not long after that I made the front page, and, even better, page three! The front page said 'Brave Nicole's date with Pop Idol!' I wish! It was about me meeting Lemar. I met him at a concert he did at Port Lymnpe Zoo to raise money for the zoo. I'm a big fan of his, and was really excited about meeting him. He was really nice and absolutely brilliant live.

Summer 2005

That summer I got several urine infections, and so while I was stuck in bed I spent a lot of time on the Internet finding out about adopting animals. I wanted to sponsor a dog and while I was researching that I found the websites of different charities of other animals that you can adopt. JAWS read the information to me and Mum described the pictures. One day I am going to have a group of adopted animals including a gorilla, an orang-utan, a chimp, dolphin, panda, tiger, elephant, donkey, horse and a tortoise. I think that's all!

Also that summer The Girls got their GCSE results. They all did brilliantly and all passed. I was really pleased for them. I was sad at the same time, though, that I wasn't getting my results along with them, but the only result I really wanted was the 'all clear'.

Back on my feet

Possibly the biggest event for me in 2005 was the operation on my feet. I'd spoken to someone the year before about getting my left foot back flat again on the floor. My leg had become tight at the back, and when I tried to walk I was walking on tiptoes. It was preventing me reaching my goal to walk. It was months before I could get an appointment but in April that year I saw Dr Gough at Guy's Hospital. He looked at both my feet and said he would operate. Although the right foot was reasonably flat, he felt it was best to do both. I'd had plastic splints made, while waiting for the operation, to help stretch the ligament back to normal, but they didn't help at all. I also started to use a standing frame at school. It was a big frame with a tray on the front. It had sides and a strap at the back that was tightened against me while I was standing to hold me up. It was to strengthen my legs, and also to see if the weight of my body would push my foot down. It was quite uncomfortable, and I could often only manage to stand for about five minutes. That was as much as I could take before my body started shaking and it began to hurt. It would have been fine if my foot was flat but because it wasn't, the left hip went up and then I used to twist a bit. I sometimes felt faint if I stood for too long and went really pale. It was because I wasn't used to standing upright. The frame didn't help at all with flattening my foot either.

After another check-up, to see if I still wanted the operation done, it was booked for September 27th. I've never looked forward to pain so much before. I did a daily countdown for about two months beforehand. I was so excited about getting it done.

After a long wait, Dr Gough performed the operation. I knew it would be uncomfortable, and that I would be in plaster for five weeks, but I was very happy to know the outcome would help me to walk again.

I arrived at Guy's Hospital the day before the operation. We hadn't been there long when I was asked by Gemma, a researcher for the BBC1 programme, *City Hospital*, if I would like to be filmed for the show. I had always wanted to have one of my operations filmed, so I said yes! That evening, when Dr Gough came to the ward to talk to me I asked him to check that I was properly asleep before he began the operation and he promised to poke me before he started. That reassured me!

The operation went well, and I wasn't in too much pain afterwards. Nick, a cameraman for *City Hospital*, filmed it. Three days after the op I was able to stand on my casts to get into my chair. I felt a bit wobbly but otherwise fine and I was surprised that there was almost no pain. I left hospital with the biggest, poshest bouquet of flowers ever – lilies, ferns, fancy leaves and my favourite flowers, gerberas – all wrapped up with a pink bow. Nick gave them to me along with signed stickers from the presenters of *City Hospital* for me to stick on my casts. Here are some of them.

To Nicole. Can't wait to meet you!! Big love, Nadia

Nicole – Happy smelly cooking, love Ainslie Harriot

Nicole – stay showbiz, love Andi Peters

To Nicole, Big Hello from Nadia's floor manager! big kisses Royston xxx

Nicole – you are a star, luv Elaine (line producer)

Dear Nicole, you are an inspiration to us all! Lots of love, Gemma xxx

I didn't waste the stickers on my casts, though! I stuck them in a special book.

I went to St Thomas's Hospital a few weeks later to be on the live show. It was a very early start – I had to be up at 5.45 a.m. – but it was worth it. I met all the presenters, and I had a great time. I had been a bit nervous, but everyone was so nice that it relaxed me. I had a slight disaster five minutes before the show started – Mum spilt tea on me! She went to pass me my tea as I went to fluff up my hair, and I knocked the cup. I couldn't believe it was my TV debut, and I looked like I'd wet myself! Luckily it didn't show though. Since then I've become quite a regular on the programme, and I love going back to see everyone.

The next day, October 14th, the first extracts from my diary were published in the *Times Educational Supplement*. There was a picture of me and the dogs on the front cover of the *TES* Friday magazine. Parts of my diary were printed in there for ten weeks. I got some great feedback on it, and I remain grateful to the *TES* Friday team for all their help.

Then on 1st November I stood on my own for thirteen seconds. I had been walking between the parallel bars and I tried to be cocky – taking one hand off the bar. Kamala, my physiotherapist, told me to take both hands off. So I did. I still had my casts on at this point, which I think helped. Although my goal had always been to walk again, that was the moment when I began to believe that it would really happen. I had thought of this quote the day before my operation, and it's what I stick to now.

'These feet are made for walking, and that's just what they'll do. One of these days these feet are gonna walk in high-heeled shoes!'

Three weeks after I had my casts taken off my legs, I went shoe shopping! I hadn't done that in three years, and *City Hospital* filmed me going round the shops. Some of my friends came too, and they helped me pick them out. It was great to get shoes on that I wouldn't have been able to wear before my operation. I got two pairs that day. I went shoe shopping again a month later. I had a lot of catching up to do! I was really excited and happy, but I ended up getting quite frustrated with trying shoes because I still couldn't get some styles on.

A few months after I'd had the casts taken off my legs, I was fitted for splints. These were hard plastic, to keep my feet in position and to stop my feet going back to the way they had been. To make the splints I had clingfilm wrapped round my legs to stop the plaster sticking, and then I had mod roc wrapped round. My foot was held in a position until the plaster had dried. A metal rod was then put between my leg and the plaster, and then a scalpel cut down the front to take them off. This was the mould. I had two pairs made – one to wear in bed, and one pair to wear in my trainers. They were a sexy leopard print! They went from just below my knee, to my toes. They covered the backs of my legs and had straps across the front to keep them in place. They really did the job as they supported my ankles well when I was walking at the gym. They could be quite uncomfortable and could dig in, but I gradually got used to them. I still use them now from time to time.

In December I went to the Philip Lawrence Awards, which are awards for young people who make a difference in their community. I won one along with three other teenagers at Demelza House for TIZ, the adolescent room we designed. We went to London the day before the awards for a practice run, and were put up in the Hilton Hotel. There was a lovely ceremony the next morning with Sir Trevor McDonald hosting it. There were ten winners from around the UK with various projects from anti-racism and bullying campaigns to youth groups and people helping the elderly. Each group won a trophy and £1,000 to help with their project.

I set up my own website in December. The address is www.c-h-o-c.org.uk, which stands for charity helping other children. It is all in pink. It started off with four links about me, Demelza, the Silver Lining Appeal and my poems, but more things have been added over the years. I do a weekly diary to let everyone know what I've been up to, and often to have a rant about things. I get quite a lot of visitors and get guest book messages from around the world. I love hearing from different people. My aims for setting up the site were to meet new people, to help with my fundraising and to let people know about my story.

I for Eileen

Auntie Eileen, my Nanny's sister, was born with cerebral palsy. When she was a little girl she wrote a book of short stories about her life. She named it *I for Eileen* because when she was at school and being taught embroidery, her teacher began to stitch the letter 'I' on the corner of a hankie. Auntie Eileen told her it should have been an 'E' but was told that it didn't matter. She never forgot that, or got her book published, so I would like to dedicate this part of my book to her. For the last forty years of her life she was in a wheelchair. She and I are very similar – so I've been told.

She died a few days before Christmas in 2001. I remember opening presents from her and looking up to the sky and saying thanks. Before she died she had said to my Nanny, Mum and Linda, 'If you ever see a white feather it will be a feather from an angel's wing and it will be a sign from me.'

Not long after she died a little white feather floated down past Mum as she was about to go through the door at work. Linda also found one which she has kept.

I think I found my first feather the day before one of my hospital visits. Mum brought the washing in and flapped out a towel and a white feather floated out. I kept it under my pillow that night.

I remember the next one quite clearly. We were in the ambulance going to the Royal Marsden Hospital for a routine six-monthly MRI scan. I was a bit nervous until Mum saw a white feather under the seat. At that exact moment, any fear that I'd had disappeared. I put the feather in my bag and went to the children's ward with a 'don't care' attitude. It was the first time a needle really didn't hurt at all. It was after that scan that I was told everything was fine and that my tumours hadn't grown. Also, what they had thought were lots of tiny tumours covering my brain and spine, were actually something called infarctions, which are little splatterings of blood caused by the haemorrhage.

I remember another occasion – my first visit to Demelza House. I was sitting on one of the sofas, nervous about what to expect. Then Mum saw a white feather on the sofa opposite. That relaxed me and I've loved Demelza House ever since. I've found more feathers, and they always seem to be at a significant time.

I don't know if I actually believe that they have been sent from Auntie Eileen but I like to think so. I think Auntie Eileen is my guardian angel who pulled me through when I was so ill. She had died the Christmas before, which can't have helped Mum, as she watched my body shut down and give up just like hers had done.

When I'm an angel my wings are going to be pink. I will send pink feathers as my sign.

The New Life of
Nicole Dryburgh . . .

2006

The year 2005 ended on a high with my operation, and I was excited about what I was going to be able to do in 2006. I had lots of ideas and goals for the future.

Topshop 'til you drop!

I had a session with a stylist at Topshop. I'd been stopped the week before in Topshop to say they had a new stylist in the store, who styled people for free. I didn't know whether to be offended that they'd stopped me or not, but it sounded fun. I booked an appointment, and Mum and I went. The stylist had her own little room in the shop with a changing-room and clothes rail. I'd told her the week before what kind of style I wanted, so she had a range of clothes ready for me to try. If we needed it in a different colour or size then she got it. It was great for Mum because she didn't have to go round the shop for me and describe everything as usual. I spent about an hour and a half with the stylist, and I ended up buying practically everything she showed me. It was great fun, and the next week I went back to get accessories!

We had a 'posh nosh' weekend at Demelza in February. I started off by eating pizza from the box. Very posh! Four officials from the Tower of London came to talk to us. I tried on some armour and got to feel the crown jewels, quite literally! A Beefeater called Richard was really nice and funny. He had his uniform on and let me feel it. I felt the medals and the embroidery on his chest. He said, 'You're not feeling any more,' and I said, 'I don't want to!' I hope he wasn't too offended!

I was given a pink plastic tiara on the Friday night which I wore all night and all day Saturday (apart from when I wore the real crown), and I even wore it to the pub on Saturday night and halfway round Blockbusters. We were recommended to rent *Deuce Bigalow*. For those who have seen it, they will know that it's quite rude. I can't say too much as I don't know who's reading this but someone had to do some very interesting describing for me! I'd just like to add that it was an adolescent weekend!

Step by step

From the start of 2006 I made a lot of progress at the gym. I was beginning to use the muscles in my legs a lot more, and not rely on my arms as much. I could stand unaided for ten seconds which was a big achievement. I walked in the parallel bars, rode on the exercise bike, walked on the treadmill, used the trampoline and walked round the gym with a walking frame. I did a little bit more each time I went. I found a trolley in the cupboard at the gym one day, like the kind grannies push, and fell in love with it! It had a little basket at the front and a seat to sit on if you got tired! It was really easy to push, and I used to walk round the gym a lot with it. It didn't do much for my street cred though!

Then in April I walked in the hydrotherapy pool unaided! My physiotherapist said to me, 'I'll have you walking unaided in five weeks' time.' I didn't think it was possible, but I did it in three weeks! The hydro pool has bars on the sides, and I stood in front of the bar. I took three steps back, then walked forward without holding on. Then I took four steps back, and walked forward. I gradually took more and more steps back until I was walking the full length of the pool, which is seventeen steps! It felt great, but also quite scary and strange. I couldn't walk in a straight line, and kept walking into the wall, but I got better with practice.

It's all *OK!*

This year one of my dreams came true. I was in *OK!* magazine! I was invited to a charity rock concert through *City Hospital*, in aid of the Evelina Children's Hospital at Guy's and St Thomas's. Acts like Robert Plant and Lulu were performing. I met Lulu before the concert started, which was great and I thought that would be the highlight of my night. Half an hour later I was queuing for a hot dog when a lady said that she recognised me from *City Hospital* and that I was an inspiration. I was so shocked and chuffed that I was at a star-studded party, and *I* had been recognised. Mum and I went back to our table, and were still talking about it, when the lady, Renee, came over and introduced us to her husband Stan – the managing director of *OK!* magazine. I was gobsmacked, but so pleased to meet him. We chatted for quite a while. Stan then went away and came back with Katie Price and Peter Andre! I'm a big fan of Katie's and she was lovely to meet. Stan also brought over Mohamed Al Fayed, who gave me a hug and offered me lunch and shopping at Harrods! I just couldn't believe what was happening. People were walking past me and looking as if to say, 'Who is she?' I just kept smiling. The concert was brilliant and I met loads of new people. Stan asked one of his photographers to take lots of photos of me with people and said he would put me in the magazine. True to his word, a few weeks later, I appeared with Lulu on page 155 of *OK!* magazine. That had been on my list of goals to achieve.

I went to see Take That at Wembley Arena. It was the best concert I've ever been to. Mum didn't have to tell me when they came on stage, because the noise nearly burst my eardrums, and I'm not exaggerating! I was a massive Take That fan when I was little. I was even bribed once by Lesley to eat my roast dinners for a month to get a duvet cover with them on! I was a Gary Barlow fan and had a badge the size of my head with his face on! At the concert he waved at me, but obviously I didn't know, so I ignored him! Mum got my hand and started flapping it, and I wondered what she was doing! They sang all the classics, and it was just brilliant.

I opened a new section of my local Asda! Demelza House was asked if they knew someone who would like to open it and they said they knew the perfect person! That morning they were also raising money for Demelza. They got a pink ribbon, at my request, for me to cut, and had pink balloons too. I cut the ribbon and everyone clapped. I was given a bouquet of flowers and vouchers for the store. I felt like a celebrity for five minutes. I was also booked for my next event, which was to cut the cake at a bus rally later on in the year, also in aid of Demelza.

Silence for Silver

I decided at the beginning of the year to set myself a big fund-raising target. I had recently been to a party for the Silver Lining Appeal, and wanted to help them in a big way. I contacted them and told them the kind of thing I wanted to do, and they said that they needed £30,000 to equip a neuro-rehabilitation room. It was exactly the sort of thing I wanted to fund-raise for. The room will have specialist equipment to help children recover after brain and spinal injuries. The equipment includes two electric beds, multi-sensory equipment and a hoist in the ceiling to lift children from their beds to the bathroom. My first event to raise money was an Easter fair at school, which had lots of games and chocolate for the children.

My second event was a 24-hour sponsored silence. There's not much to say about it apart from the fact it was quite boring. Mum had a migraine, so spent a lot of time in bed, and I was just silent in my room. I spent a lot of time on my laptop and texting – was that cheating? Anyway, I did it and didn't speak once. Well maybe once, but it wasn't my fault. Mum told me to turn *Hollyoaks* down and I shouted, 'Yeah,' to let her know I'd heard her. I forgot I wasn't supposed to speak, but apart from that I was totally silent. I had a whistle which I blew when I wanted Mum's attention. Then I used my own special sign language to say what I wanted. In the end the silence was longer than 24 hours. It lasted from 10.30 p.m. on Sunday to 9 a.m. on Tuesday. I won't be doing it again!

Hickstead and Harrods

I was due to take part in my second competition at Hickstead on 8th June 2006, but three days before, I fell from my horse, Sox. I had just gone outside to the arena to practise my routine. The next thing I remember is waking up on the floor. My mind was completely blank. I couldn't feel my back, and my head was throbbing. Then I started to think that I was ruined, that everything I'd worked for during these last three years was gone – very dramatic, I know!

An ambulance was called, and slowly things started coming back to me. I remembered the date, and then what I was wearing. I was told a pigeon had spooked Sox and she had flung me off. Obviously there was no way of me seeing this coming to prevent my fall. When the ambulance came I was strapped on to a spinal board. It hurt like mad, and I was saying things out loud, which I thought I was just thinking. I kept moaning that I'd broken two nails. At the hospital I was checked over and given a CT scan, which showed that nothing was broken. I was told I wasn't allowed to take part in my competition. I was gutted. It then turned out that it wasn't a pigeon that had spooked Sox, but children playing in a bush and flicking stuff at her. She went to gallop off and I just flew backwards, and landed flat on to my back. I had to have lots of bed-rest. I'd never felt pain like it.

I rode a different horse when I went back to RDA to get used to riding again after the fall. I rode fat Ingrid. She was really slow and round. I said it was like riding a wobbly armchair. She was really polite and did as she was told – unlike Sox. Sox has attitude – my kind of girl! (And she stops when she wants to, huffs the whole way round the arena, and looks in the mirror all the time to see how pretty she is!) It was strange getting used to a different horse. It also hurt my legs more because they had to be stretched wider to fit round her! I kept panicking every time she slightly tripped because that was the movement I felt when Sox got spooked and she tried to gallop off.

I went back to the gym a few weeks after my fall, but I couldn't do what I used to be able to do. My back kept going into a really painful spasm when I lay down too flat, and sometimes while I was walking in the parallel bars. It was really frustrating. I saw my doctor about it, but I was told I just needed time.

At the end of June I flew a plane! Well, only a glider. It had been arranged through Demelza and it was so much fun. We spent the day at the gliding centre, and I went up twice. The first time the glider was pulled along the ground by a tow plane, and when we were high enough, the two planes separated. I was in the glider with another person behind me. He had controls in the back, and I had a gear-stick in the front. It was a really hot day and I had to put sun cream on because otherwise I would have got sunburnt. I was allowed to take control, and I stalled it twice. It scared me a little bit because the glider just stopped. I thought we were going to fall down, but the man behind me took over the controls again. I did lots of nosedives and rollercoaster moves. I was in the air for about half an hour. Landing was a bit bumpy. The glider has no wheels, so you literally just crash-landed. I went up again five minutes later. This time we used the winch to get up. You're basically shot up like a rocket. That was the best bit. That time I spent five minutes in the air. I wanted a glider after that, but they are quite expensive, and Mum said no!

I finally had my trip to Harrods in August. My previous trip had to be cancelled because I'd fallen off Sox, and needed time to recover. We were shown round the store by Lisa, Mr Al Fayed's PA, and taken to lunch. I had chicken nuggets and chips. Nothing changes . . . Then Mr Al Fayed came to meet us. He brought me a big Harrods bear, chocolates and perfume. He also gave me money to spend in the store. I headed straight to the pet section. That's what I had been looking forward to the most. I got Molly a Harrods collar and lead, and Daizy a designer dog bowl. I was allowed to hold a really expensive chihuahua in the pet section. I fell in love with him, but I wasn't allowed to bring him home. I also held a really cute rabbit. I had a brilliant day, and went home with lots of bags.

At the beginning of September I went to see Dr Martin. We bumped into Dr McCormick while we were there, so he came in the room with us. It was good to get both their opinions on the pain in my back, and for the other problems I had. Dr McCormick was able to compare the symptoms to the ones I had when I was eleven. I'd been getting the same kind of pain in my arm and hand like I had then. He made me do the certain stretch which I did back then and which made the pain happen, but nothing happened when I did it this time. I'd been getting a lot of pain in my knee and back too, which they put down to me doing a lot more exercise at the gym. They agreed to book me in for an MRI scan to reassure me.

After that, I went on holiday to Scotland. It was my first trip back after three years, and on that last visit I was on chemotherapy. It was great seeing everyone again, and they could see how much stronger I had become since that time. The weather was good, and it only rained once!

Back on course . . . work!

Back in March, I had suddenly been told there was a meeting the next day at Canterbury College to discuss me going there. I wasn't happy at all. I didn't want to go to college, but went along to the meeting anyway. I told them that I wanted to be a journalist and have a career in writing. They said that I couldn't do the media course because part of that involved film work, and I couldn't do that. I would be able to do the English course though, to help with my writing. There were a few more meetings over the next months where I met my English teacher. I also met my support teacher who would help me in my lessons by writing down all the notes and emailing them to me at home later.

I started college at the end of September. I wasn't happy about going at all at first and put up a fight, but then I decided I had grown out of St Nicholas' School, and I wanted to do my GCSEs. I enrolled to do English GCSE to help with a career in writing and becoming a columnist.

Back to Baldilocks

The week before I started I had the MRI scan. My back hadn't been the same since the fall in June, and I kept getting pain in my arm similar to the pain I got with my first tumour. I wasn't surprised when the results showed that my cancer had come back. Both my tumours had started growing again. Mum found out a couple of days before me. I was in Birmingham for the weekend with Demelza and twenty other past winners, sorting through the nominations for the year's Philip Lawrence awards, and she didn't want to ruin it. I came back from a brilliant weekend to discover the news.

Less than eighteen hours after finding out, I was in my oncologist, Darren Hargrave's room. I hoped I'd never see him again, but I mean that in the nicest possible way. He explained that there was a definite enlargement in both my tumours. He didn't know for how long they'd been growing again, or if the fall from Sox had triggered them off. We discussed treatment, for which chemo was the only option. I'd had the maximum dose of radiotherapy to the top of my spine for my first tumour, and surgery was too risky because the tumours were too wrapped round my spine. I was quite shocked to hear that the first lot of chemo I had, when I was fourteen, only had a 30 per cent chance of working. I hadn't known that – it had never occurred to me to ask. Darren said, 'Look what you've done on 30 per cent.' That helped me. The new chemo had a 60 per cent chance of working.

I was fine talking about everything until it got to the part about blood transfusions. I found it really hard to get my head around the fact that I would have to have someone else's blood in me. We discussed the treatment and the side effects. I left feeling a bit better than when I arrived. I delayed starting the treatment for a week because I had been selected to be a judge on the panel for the Philip Lawrence Awards to pick the final winners, and it meant going to London for the day and being on the panel with Sir Trevor McDonald. I didn't want to be ill for that, and we didn't know how quickly

I would be affected by the chemo.

On 12th October I had a Hickman line fitted. It's a tube that comes out from the stomach and all chemo and medicines are given through this, including blood tests. It meant I didn't have to worry about needles. I started my chemotherapy the same night I had the line fitted. I was told it would be a much tougher ride this time, which I expected anyway. I had four days of intravenous chemotherapy, and then was allowed home. My hair fell out more quickly than I had remembered it doing the last time – all had gone within two weeks. I went into hospital with an infected Hickman line and a full head of perfect curls, and came out five days later being able to count the hairs left on my head. It had all got matted, and was really painful. It was itchy too and I made bald patches by scratching my head and the hair snapping from the root. It was really sore as well because I kept scratching bare skin. Mum had to cut my hair while I was in hospital to get rid of the heavy mass, and someone had to bring me a hat to go home in. The first month of treatment was the worst. My line got infected, and it was so painful. I had a high temperature and I had to have my first blood transfusion. That was the part of the treatment I hadn't liked the sound of. I had sore spots covering my head and ulcers and sores in my mouth. I had to take liquid morphine for the pain.

I found out lots of new things about chemo that I hadn't had to deal with the first time round. For example, what neutropenic meant (it's when your immune system and blood counts are low, so I had to keep away from anyone with any 'lurgy'), and the different parts of the blood. I had four days of chemo every three weeks at the Royal Marsden. The week after chemo was normally good, but then after that I would get a high temperature and end up in my local hospital. It was normally due to a urine infection, or an infected Hickman line.

When I found out I had relapsed I got in touch with *City Hospital*, to see if they would film my journey. I wanted to show what it is like to go through chemotherapy, and how you can still get on with life while you're having it. They agreed and gave us a video camera to do a home diary. Sometimes the last thing I wanted was a camera in my face when I was feeling so ill, but it also helped to have a rant on film. I'm really glad now that I filmed my journey, because it shows how far I've come.

On November 1st I made a speech at the House of Lords! It was about 'Move' – a physio programme I do. It's for children with disabilities. All the children have their own goals to reach and little targets to achieve on the way. My goal was to walk by Christmas with Mum on one side and a stick on the other. That had to be put on hold due to chemo. I did 'Move' at school, so a few of us went to the House of Lords in a minibus. There were lots of lords, ladies, professors and official people there. We all mingled and had food and drink for about an hour before the speeches began. A Disability Rights Commissioner spoke first, followed by a children's paediatrician, then the head teacher from our school, St Nicholas', our school, the mother of one of the children who is doing the 'Move' programme, and last but not least was me! I had written a speech but the week before the event I went into hospital with a high temperature, and was only let out at 11 p.m. the night before, so I had absolutely no idea what I was going to say, but I just spoke. I think I did OK, but there's loads now I wish I'd said. Afterwards Mum told me there were about 130 people in the room. I was given a lovely big bouquet of pink flowers and Lemar's new album. It was my first speech. What a way to start!

Just before I started my chemotherapy I got in touch with the *Whitstable Gazette*, to see if they knew anyone who would like me to write a column for them about my treatment. They said they would, so from the start of October 2006, I have written a weekly column for them. I love doing it and have had some great feedback on it. It also meant that I achieved another one of my goals – to become a columnist.

I went back to college in October after four weeks off. Everyone in my class had found out by this time what was wrong with me, which I didn't mind. The class was half the size of when we started because a lot of people had dropped out. We started to learn Shakespeare's *Othello*, which I didn't understand at all. We watched a video, but it was as if it was in a foreign language. I actually started to like college a bit then because it gave me something to take my mind off chemo. I started to get coursework, which I hadn't had for four years! When I was too ill to go to the lessons my support teacher went and wrote down the notes for me. She then emailed them to me at home.

I tried to keep up with my exercises while I was in hospital. During my second round of chemo I went along to the hospital gym. I couldn't do much because I was connected to the drips, and I was paranoid about tugging on my Hickman line and pulling it out. While I was lying on the bench doing my exercises I found two feathers. I hadn't found one for several years. I believe they were from Auntie Eileen and Wes, my friend from Demelza who had passed away the day before. The physiotherapist had worked there for eight years, and had never found a feather in the gym. I just knew I was supposed to go to the gym that day. It made me feel calm and more positive about my treatment.

As soon as I was disconnected from my drips after my third round of chemo at the end of November, I started to get a pain in my right arm. It felt really bruised and sore. It was gradually getting worse, but I thought I just needed to get home to rest. It took three hours to get home from the Marsden, and by the time I got into the house I was in agony. When I took my jacket off and Mum looked at my arm, it was double its usual size and a mottled blue colour. Mum phoned the on-call nurse, and she said it sounded like a blood clot, and that I needed to go straight to our local hospital. I wasn't happy, as I had been looking forward to sleeping in my own bed that night. I had a blood sample taken which showed there was a clot. They couldn't find it when they did an ultrasound though. They started treating me for a clot. I began having daily injections to thin my blood. I tried Warfarin tablets so I could stop the injections, but I bled too much, so had to keep having them. I was devastated when I was told I needed to have a daily injection for at least three months. I had to stay in hospital for about five days. It took three days before my arm stopped hurting so much. I couldn't move or do anything with it. I was paranoid about my arm for months, and kept asking Mum to check what colour and size it was.

Because I had to have an injection every day, it was

too much for the community nurses to come out or for us to go to hospital, so Mum had to learn how to do it. It was really hard for me to let her, but she didn't do too bad the first time. I knew I had to let her do it, but I hadn't planned it for that day and had to be talked into it. We discussed it for half an hour with my nurse, which just made it worse because I then knew what was going to happen. I had the injection in my stomach, so I had to try and not wobble my belly through crying while she was doing it. It actually made it a lot easier having Mum do it because I got used to the one person. Also I could be injected wherever we went because it had to be done at the same time every day, and before Mum learnt we had to be home by 3 p.m. and that normally interfered with our plans for the day.

I had an MRI scan on 11th December 2006. It showed the tumours had stayed the same size, and the chemo was working. Before each course of the chemo I've had to have an echo scan of my heart and a kidney test as one of the chemos is known for damaging parts of these. Sometimes I couldn't have as high a dose of chemo as I should have because my heart or kidneys weren't strong enough, so the dose was slightly reduced.

14th December 2006

Today was the fourth anniversary of my brain haemorrhage. It doesn't seem that long. I can't believe I've been blind and disabled for four years, but look how far I've come since that day.

I am halfway through my chemo. I don't know what the future really holds. I still have my dreams and goals, but most of them have just had to be put on hold for a while. I have achieved three of my goals though – to become a columnist, to be in *OK!* magazine and to walk, even though it was only in the hydro pool.

Mum is fine. We still get on really well and have a laugh. She's having to put up with my mood swings through chemo. I have got quite aggressive and obsessive about food. Lee has had to go out and get me the food when I have wanted it. I have not been satisfied unless it's been a specific thing from a specific place!

Molly is still lovely, calm and cute, and Daizy is well . . . Daizy – just the way I like her!

Eighteen at Last!

It wasn't until six weeks before our birthdays that Lee and I finally decided to organise the joint 18th/21st party that we had been looking forward to for years. In the months leading up to it we had thought that I would be too ill – or in hospital – to have one. In January I went shopping for my birthday outfit – I planned the trip on a good week of my chemo cycle. I managed to find my outfit in the first two shops I went in, which for me was brilliant! I knew in my mind what I wanted. The colour theme of the party was pink and black, so it had to be those colours. I got black trousers, and a pink strappy top, with the bust covered in sequins. It was exactly what I wanted, and it meant I could then relax knowing that I had it.

I had been diagnosed with scoliosis in March 2006. I've always had a bit of a curve in my spine, but it had got worse. The first appointment I could get to see a specialist was January 2007! He said that it wasn't that bad – only 40 degrees out – and to just leave it for now, and see if it gets any worse, but it probably won't because I shouldn't grow any more.

Towards the end of my chemotherapy treatment I really had to concentrate on my coursework for college. I went in for some extra lessons when I was well enough, to talk about things I had missed or didn't understand. I had to do a presentation on a subject of my choice, and I chose Demelza House. I got an A* for it, so I was really pleased with that. I spent ages doing essays and was so relieved when I finished them, but I did get quite stressed while doing them.

The chemo was much tougher than I had expected. By the fourth round I'd had enough and was totally fed up. It felt like I was spending more time in hospital than out. The hardest part was being away from the dogs. I missed them so much. I got quite stressed while on chemo because I couldn't plan things, and other things I had planned I had to cancel. It was so boring in hospital because there was nothing for me to do but listen to the radio. I was shocked at how obsessive chemo made me about food. I was trying new foods, which isn't like me at all. My craving this time round was chicken in spicy breadcrumbs, and sweet and sour chicken balls. I was really hungry the week I had chemo, but ate normally the next week, and wasn't that hungry the week after that, then it was back to hungry week. My weight didn't really change, but I lost a little bit. I used to throw hissy fits about stupid things, and my mood was up and down a lot. I had a headache most of the time, felt really weak and tired, bruised a lot and generally felt rubbish. My Hickman line was really temperamental and it sometimes took an hour and a half to make it work. I was threatened so many times with a blood test in my arm to get a sample, but I was adamant they used my line. I found that I had to hold my arm up in a certain position to make the blood come out. After trying for an hour once to make it work I got so fed up that I puffed really loudly, and the blood flowed out! I used that trick from then on to make it work.

I got really annoyed with the staff in one of the hospitals I had to stay at regularly. The first time I had to stay there for a few days, they didn't even read my notes properly to know that I was blind and disabled! I lost count too of the amount of times that a doctor or nurse came in my room while I had friends and family there, and just started talking about my private details. I was given no respect or dignity at all. There are so many stories I could tell, but I would be here all day.

I was due to have my sixth and final round of chemo the week before my birthday, but I asked if it could be delayed for two weeks. I had worked out the cycle by this time – I felt fine for a week, but then became neutropenic and felt awful and would end up in hospital. If I'd had my chemo the week I was supposed to, I would have been in no mood to party on my eighteenth, so my oncologist agreed to delay it until a few days after our party. It also meant I had a longer time to pick up from the previous round and feel great for my birthday.

I made a lot of progress with my fund-raising for the Silver Lining Appeal during chemo. People were really generous and organised events to raise money. I had a target to raise £5,000 by my eighteenth, which I reached on my birthday when my grandad gave me £250, which was what I needed to reach the £5,000 mark. I thought on my birthday that I hadn't reached my goal, so I was really pleased when I opened the card from Grandad. I thought my fund-raising would have to stop for a while so I was really touched that other people organised events for me to help me reach my £30,000 target.

I was very precise in what I wanted at the party, from the colour theme and decorations, to the food. I made sure Lee was happy with the plans as well. I was at Demelza the weekend before, so I could celebrate there with my friends. They had decorated my room with lots of balloons and streamers. Mum did the food shopping for the party while I was away. I gave her a list of what I wanted. She got that plus more! All the food was colour co-ordinated. There were pink wafer biscuits, pink marshmallows, rainbow drops, iced gems, party rings, pink and black sweets, pink coconut-covered chocolate marshmallows and lots more.

I had my brace taken off three days before my birthday. I had a porcelain brace fitted to my top teeth the summer before. It had taken a long time to find a dentist who would agree to give me a porcelain one because they are more expensive. I couldn't have a normal metal one because of the MRI scans. Each bracket was white porcelain, the only metal being the thin wire. You could hardly notice it. I was amazed at how fast it worked, and I was able to have the brace taken off just before my birthday. I now have my perfect smile.

I woke up at about 8.30 a.m. on my birthday. I opened some of my presents and cards. I had asked for a silver charm bracelet from Mum. She got me one with the number '18' charm on it.

Most of the day was spent getting the hall ready by setting up the tables with pink tablecloths and napkins, bowls of sweets, confetti, and putting up bunting and embarrassing photos of Lee and me etc.

We had a lot of friends and family come down from Scotland for our party. Mum's friend, Gloria, is a brilliant balloon modeller, and did the balloons for the hall. There were singing balloons, a 3-D Tinkerbell helium balloon, helium cocktail glasses, pink and black balloons attached together to make palm trees, and lots more.

My friend Frances, who is a professional make-up artist, did my make-up. It was really natural. She had to stick false eyelashes on because I had lost mine through chemo, which felt really strange. She also pencilled in my eyebrows because I had lost them too. I had a long pink wig with black streaks which matched my outfit. Everyone turned up in pink and black – even the boys!

I got so many presents that I had to stop opening them at the party on the night. Everyone had made such an effort with wrapping the presents in pink and black, and most of my cards had things on that I could feel. A lot of people got me charms for my bracelet to remind me of them. I spent the beginning of the night saying hello to everyone, then sat at a table with Kerry, Charlotte, Rachel, Nicola and Nick, the cameraman from *City Hospital*. He came to film it, and he is also a good friend of mine now. We had a ridiculous amount of empty bottles and glasses on our table – only some of them were mine. Near the end of the night the DJ played the cancan song, so Lee took me on to the dance floor and moved my chair about, while I held hands with some of The Girls and danced. Lee organised the music. His friend was our DJ and he played a range of music to keep all ages happy.

Two of my friends prepared the food. We had home-made pizza, potato wedges, sausage rolls and chicken goujons. We had a chocolate fountain with fruit, flapjacks and marshmallows to dip in, plus little fairy cakes with pink and black icing and decorations that I designed. Another friend made our birthday cakes. I had a fantastic pink handbag cake with a big buckle on the front, and Lee had a male torso with a six-pack with bling!

We got home at 1 a.m., but stayed up until 4 a.m. chatting with friends. I had a brilliant night.

It was the day only I had ever believed I'd get to see.

There are some things I'd like people to take from my story:

Never take anything for granted. When you next get up and walk to the kitchen for something, remember I can't do that, along with every other disabled person. Appreciate it.

When you're reading this book, remember I can't. I'll have to have it read to me. Hopefully it will be recorded one day.

When you look at photos of friends and family and at yourself in the mirror, remember I can't do that either. I'll never know what a grown-up me looks like. I can only imagine.

And when you breathe in and out, remember I *can* do that, because I'm still here and fighting.

I have dreams and goals:

I would like to become a columnist in either a magazine or newspaper.

I'd like to design fashionable clothes for wheelchair users, none of those big old granny skirts. (No offence, Grannies!)

I'd also like to design T-shirts with cheeky slogans for teenagers with disabilities to wear when other people stare at us.

I'd like to become a songwriter.

I want to continue my charity work and hope to have my own charity one day.

I'm one stubborn, determined little madam – I won't stop until I've reached my goals.

I wouldn't really want to change my life now. This has happened to me for a reason. I may not be what you would call your average teenager but I'm doing things I never would have done if I were normal. I don't let my disabilities stop me from doing things.

I'm not ashamed of who I am or what I've been through. Maybe I would wish not to be disabled or blind but I would never change the fact that I have cancer. No one can deny the fact that it is what has made me who I am, given me my personality and my need to succeed. It's made me a fighter and given me strength. It made me realise what's important and what's not. I will continue fighting and proving people wrong. It's what I was born to do! You haven't heard the last of me.

Love Nicole xxx

The Facts

Nicole asked her oncologist six months before her relapse in 2006 to explain some of the medical facts about her tumours.

Dear Nicole

A peripheral nerve sheath tumour (PNST) consists of tumours arising from a peripheral nerve. PNSTs may be subdivided into benign and malignant (MPNST) – cancerous – variants.

The incidence of MPNST is in general low, but half of all cases arise in patients with the hereditary disorder Neurofibromatosis type 1 *(NF1). I don't have figures but MPNSTs are very rare in someone like you, Nicole, who does not have NF1.*

All ages and both sexes may be affected by PNSTs. Sporadic (this is you, Nicole, as you do not have NF1) MPNSTs are most common between 40 and 50 years of age, while those occurring in the setting of NF1 are diagnosed some 10 years earlier.

In total, MPNSTs account for 5–10% of all soft tissue sarcomas.

Your second tumour was due to the first one not being completely killed by the radiotherapy and seeding to the rest of your spinal cord (this was proven by Chris Chandler's biopsy), we also thought it had gone to your brain but we now doubt this as the abnormal areas may have been due to your stroke (bleed).

Usually a malignant (cancerous) tumour such as MPNST that has relapsed and spread throughout the spinal cord should not be able to be cured by chemotherapy! We decided to use a lower dose chemotherapy that you took by mouth and obviously it surprised us in that it stopped the tumour from growing and your previous MRI scans show that the tumour was static (i.e. not bigger or smaller). We do not know from the scans whether it is dead or not but the chemotherapy at least has switched it off. The big question is for how long? Could it be that we have cured you (possibly, and the chance gets greater the longer you are well) but there is a chance it could grow back again.

If it did grow back I would be keen to offer more treatment though!

Darren

Dr McCormick sent the following explanation of his involvement with Nicole and his role at King's College Hospital.

I moved jobs from Kent and Canterbury Hospital to King's College Hospital in February 2003, and I remember seeing you on Lion Ward in January 2003 when I came to visit. I remember meeting with your mum with Chris and

Dr Hargrave when I first started in this job to tell her about the spread of your tumour – that was very hard.

I've since had lots of discussions with Chris and Dr Hargrave about you, and we've all been amazed at how well you've been doing, appearing to go into complete remission, and making great steps with your independence despite your blindness. I have been sorry that I haven't been able to still see you now that my job has changed, but now I am spending most of my time looking after children on Lion Ward with Chris, and seeing them for follow-up afterwards here at King's.

King's College Hospital is a regional neurosurgical centre for both adults and children. The neurosurgeons here provide a service for both planned and emergency neurosurgery to a population of more than four million people. We have ten paediatric neurosurgical beds at King's College Hospital and it is therefore one of the biggest paediatric neurosurgical centres in the country. The neurosurgeons are extremely skilled at performing life-saving operations, but often the children who present to us with brain tumours, brain haemorrhages or other forms of acquired brain injury need a great deal of additional input after they have had their neurosurgery. This is where I come in.

Neuro-rehabilitation involves helping a child or young person to regain as many functions as possible after they have had their neurosurgery or acute management of their acquired brain injury. Sometimes it is possible to help the child or young person to get back completely to where they were before they came to us. Other times, they need to be helped to adapt to a significant change in their ability, such as having impaired vision or impaired movement, or sometimes even impaired thinking or learning. I like helping in this process as it is great to be part of a team who work very closely together with a child or young person's best interests at heart. Here at King's we have a fabulous team of paediatric physiotherapists, occupational therapists, speech and language therapists, psychologists, psychiatrists, dieticians, play specialists, nurses and doctors who work really well together and who love joining forces to help the patient make progress. I also like this form of work because it is very satisfying to come into what can be a very difficult situation and help the patient and their parents see that real progress can be made. I enjoy getting to know the child or young person over a period of time and continuing that relationship on as I follow them up in the Outpatient Department.

Whilst we have the staff to help this process, we are often limited by lack of equipment. Specialist equipment means that our rehabilitation efforts can be much more sophisticated and can be adapted much more to each patient's individual needs. Fund-raising is really vital if we *are able to get the equipment that we feel would be best for this purpose; the National Health Service is only able to afford equipment at a basic level and we want the very best for our patients. For instance, just one bed for a specialist neuro-rehabilitation suite costs more than £12,000! Without the fund-raising efforts of helpful individuals and companies, we would not be able to carry out the neuro-rehabilitation work to the high standard that we want. When our paediatric neuro-rehabilitation suite opens at King's, we will be the first acute inpatient dedicated neuro-rehabilitation unit in the National Health Service in the United Kingdom and we want to start as we mean to go on, that is as a top-class service.*

The Way Other People See It

Sue was a community children's nurse based in Canterbury. She remembers Nicole as a reserved, shy girl when she was first ill and receiving radiotherapy at the Royal Marsden Hospital in 2000. She was shocked when, two years later, she learned that Nicole had suffered a brain haemorrhage which had left her blind.

When Nicole was transferred back to Kent and Canterbury Hospital, our team was very aware of the extra sensitivity required when nursing a blind person. Unless people talked and explained their every move, Nicole would not know what was going on. She was in a lot of pain at this stage and very frightened. Nicole's four school friends were marvellously supportive and visited her regularly in hospital. It must have been a scary experience for them too.

Two months later when Nicole was discharged, the doctors had painted a very bleak picture. Jackie, Nicole's mum, was told there was a rumour going round school that Nicole had gone home and would probably die within two weeks – which was not the case.

Jackie was concerned about Nicole's school friends and wanted them spoken to truthfully. Arrangements were made for a colleague and myself to meet the four girls with their mums and the head of year. I felt dreadful walking into that room, seeing those frightened faces probably already realising we were going to give them bad news. We explained that Nicole was likely to die in the next six months. It was a very difficult and distressing meeting. I will always remember those girls' distraught faces.

The following week my colleague and I were asked to speak to Nicole, and to be honest with her about the apparent situation. This was very hard for her and her mum, and also for us. We told her she would not see again and that she was unlikely to walk again without a lot of help. Understandably she didn't want to hear these harsh words. But equally it was important for her to know what was going on, so she had the opportunity to make choices about what she wanted to do. She and her friends would be able to maintain an open and honest friendship. My colleague then asked Nicole whether there was anything really special that she would like to do. Tears started rolling down her cheeks, and she said she knew what we were getting at. It was a very distressing conversation to have with anyone, but particularly with a teenage girl.

I returned to their home later that day to ask if she had any more questions. Nicole was quiet but in control. I remember saying that she had the best thing to fight the cancer – her determination and spirit.

What an inspirational young lady Nicole is! Having

accepted her situation she has got on with her life and achieved a huge amount in a short space of time. No longer a quiet, shy, retiring child, Nicole is now a beautiful young lady, with a remarkably positive personality that gives her family and friends the strength to support her so readily. She exudes confidence, humour and happiness whilst also showing great consideration for others. It is a privilege to know her. Her family and friends must all be so proud of her.

Hilary was Nicole's English teacher. They met in January 2005.

I met Nicole on January 6th 2005 at the East Kent Hospital School. When I'd received a telephone call just before Christmas asking me if I knew of anyone who would be able to give English support to a young girl – in remission from cancer, blind and in a wheelchair – who was writing a diary of her experience, I'd put myself forward. I'm so glad I did.

Nicole has a wonderful sense of humour and a generous spirit; she is always thinking of others and is an indefatigable fund-raiser. When I asked her once what she would do with lots of money, she listed things she would buy her brother, Lee, and her mother, Jackie, who shares a very special relationship with Nicole.

Passionate about animals, Nicole would have a zoo if she could but contents herself with Molly and Daizy – two crazy, adorable dogs who have stayed close to Nicole through thick and thin, like the true friends they are.

Nicole had her feet straightened before Christmas – the operation was televised – and she is learning to walk again. A couple of weeks ago she invited Evelyn, Nicole's IT teacher, and me to go to the gym to watch her practise walking between parallel bars. Her physiotherapist, at some point in the proceedings, indicated that Nicole had probably done enough as she looked a bit pale and had possibly reached her limit. Nicole replied that she always pushed herself beyond her limit and she continued to walk some more. I admire her so much and the more I get to know Nicole, the more I am overwhelmed by her courage and determination.

Julie is Nicole's mum's cousin. She lives just round the corner. Julie doesn't mind driving in London and has often driven Nicole and her mother to appointments.

I awoke on Christmas morning 2002 with a feeling of sadness and unease, the same feeling I had had since Nicole collapsed on 14th December. Her condition seemed to be worsening and it looked like she was slipping into a coma.

My children were twelve and nine at the time. I remember sitting watching them open their presents thinking of the contrast at that moment between myself and Jackie, Nicole's mother, who would be sitting by her daughter's bedside willing her to live.

I managed not to cry, which for anyone who knows me, was quite a feat, until I opened my present from my great friend Sarah. Sarah and I have been through a lot together, including regular trips up to Great Ormond Street for her son Jack when he was diagnosed with a tumour on his kidney. Thankfully Jack is OK. Sarah had bought me a silver wish box which contained a piece of rose quartz for love and friendship, and three tiny 'wish' scrolls. The idea is to write a wish on each scroll, roll them up and place them back in the box and wait for your wishes to come true. Of course Nicole was my first thought. I wished for her simply to get better. I then wrote down my other two wishes and closed the box.

About half an hour later I took our boxer dog, Fred, out. As I was walking by the sea, my mind never far from Nicole, I received a text stating Nicole had woken up and spoken! Words will never be able to describe my feelings at that moment, but for me, that Christmas morning, I believed our family had been granted a Christmas miracle and of course I cried out of sheer joy!

Nicole is a fighter which is why she is here today, a true inspiration to everyone she meets, and I am so proud to know her.

Linda is Nicole's aunt, her mother's older sister. She lives quite nearby. During Nicole's stay in hospital, Linda regularly drove many of her friends and family – and, of course, Molly – to visit her.

I will never forget the day that we were told Nicole was going to die.

Since coming back to Kent and Canterbury Hospital from King's, Nicole had been deteriorating and just wasn't eating. She had never been a very good eater, even when she was well. Since starting the chemo, she just couldn't face anything. Some days she only managed a few bites of a Tuc biscuit. I could see that she was getting very weak.

Mum phoned me and said that she had had a phone call and could we go into the hospital as they wanted to talk to us. I dropped everything and jumped in the car. I'm not too sure what I thought on the way there, so many things were racing through my mind.

Jackie met us, along with Sue (the community nurse),

and we went to a parents' room along the corridor. Jackie didn't say anything at all but she obviously knew what Sue was going to tell us.

Sue told us that Nicole was very ill and we really had to prepare ourselves. She said that she and the other community nurses had worked with other children in the same condition and in their opinion she wouldn't get better. She said that there was a chance that she wouldn't live till Easter. I was desperately trying to think how long it was till Easter. It was very difficult to take in what she was saying. I was just numb.

All Nicole wanted to do was go home and Sue said that they were going to hurry through an order for a hospital bed to be delivered to Jackie's house. I can remember thinking that they were sending her home to die.

When we left the room, we went to Nicole's bedside and spoke to her before we left. It was a blessing that Nicole couldn't see our faces. We chatted and tried to behave as if everything was normal. I wonder, though, if the wobble in our voices gave the game away.

I drove home in a daze, tears streaming down my face, and thought about Jackie and how she was going to cope. That night, as I sat down to dinner with my family, I told them that Nicole was probably going to die.

Lesley is Nicole's other aunt – her mum's younger sister. She lives in Scotland and keeps in close touch.

Being so far away in Scotland I had to rely on phone calls from my mother or from my sister, Linda, updating me on Nicole's progress. Whilst they were travelling back and forth to London or looking after my nephew, Lee, and Nicole's dog, Molly, I could do nothing but wait for the daily phone call. I felt useless and just wished I could be there. While my sister Jackie keeps everything to herself, I'm the opposite, and talking to my friends and family helped me feel less isolated. Every day someone would ask, 'How's Nicole?' and even now friends that I haven't seen for a while don't enquire about me, but ask about Nicole!

After weeks of being on red alert – every time the phone rang, your stomach lurched in case it was bad news – Nicole finally came out of high dependency and was put back in a children's ward in King's College Hospital. Jackie was able to arrange for me to go and stay in the hospital with her and Nicole for a few days, something that is normally only allowed for parents.

Although they hadn't ruled out the possibility of Nicole's sight returning, it seemed more and more unlikely. They still did not know what was wrong with her and the threat of another seizure was a strong possibility. She had nearly died in hospital twice already and everyone just wanted to know what was wrong.

As I travelled to London to see Nicole and Jackie, I could not help feeling nervous. I was desperate to see them both but was worried about letting my emotions take over and breaking down. I felt that I had no right to get upset in front of Jackie and Nicole as they were the ones trying to deal with everything and I didn't want my own feelings and fears to cause them more upset.

When I went into the hospital and saw Nicole for the first time it was hard, but Nicole's sense of humour and outspokenness made it easy to forget how ill she was. Staying with her and Jackie for those few days, and becoming involved for a short while in their world, is something that I will always be grateful for.

At the end of my visit, Nicole's surgeon came to see her, and while he laughed and joked with Nicole and tried to answer her questions, I was aware of him looking at me. Nothing was said but I felt as if he was trying to gauge whether I realised how serious the situation was. I had to go home that day and the next day Nicole was to discover that the mass of blood vessels on the base of her spine was not an 'AVM' but a cancerous tumour that was growing at an alarming rate.

The way that Jackie, Nicole and Lee have dealt with Nicole's illness has made me so proud of them all.

Nanny lives fifteen minutes away from Nicole. She helped keep the family in touch with her grand-daughter's progress, looked after Lee, and was a regular visitor to the hospital.

Where do I start to talk about my granddaughter, Nicole? She was such a bubbly girl at eleven, doing her gymnastics, full of life, looking forward to the future, when it all went wrong. It was a terrible shock to be told she had cancer.

After an operation and radiotherapy she went back to school and was her old self again but a bigger shock was to come. In December 2002 she collapsed with a brain haemorrhage. I think this was the worst time, not knowing if she would come out of her coma. When I got the call on Christmas Eve to say she had woken up, it was the best news I'd ever had and a lovely Christmas present. Then being told a week later she had lost her sight was very sad and a terrible blow.

But with all the ups and downs over the last couple of years – losing her lovely hair through the chemo, learning to walk – she has been so strong. She has achieved so much with her writing and raising money for her charities.

I am so proud of her, as is everyone who knows her. She is an inspiration to us all.

Julian Gugenheim was Nicole's science teacher at Barton Court Grammar School.

I had just started my teaching career when I had heard that it would be a few weeks before one girl in my Year 7 science class would be joining us. Apparently she was having radiotherapy for a tumour that had been diagnosed just as she was finishing primary school. I sent work home for her but often wondered about this pupil who, if things had been different, would be filling the gap in my classroom.

Coincidentally another class also included a girl who was recovering from chemotherapy. It became apparent to me that for some pupils school was not going to be the biggest challenge of their young lives.

Eventually Nicole Dryburgh returned to school. Year 7 rapidly became Year 8 and I was again appointed her science teacher. Nearly a year had passed since she had received treatment and I felt it was time to treat her exactly like the others. It was probably a bit of a shock for Nicole and she rebelled against the added pressure. That, as I have discovered since, is how Nicole reacts in those circumstances. Throughout the year she frustrated the hell out of me and as a result I got to know her mum!

Nicole reached Year 9 and, probably to her relief, I was not her science teacher . . . I was her Year Co-ordinator instead! It was that December that Nicole was rushed to hospital. We knew she had lost her eyesight and that she had subsequently had a serious reaction to a drug she was given, but we did not know for sure what the diagnosis was and the details were sketchy. We could only assume it was related to her cancer two and half years earlier.

Her school friends were very concerned but none of the staff at Barton Court could reassure them with any specific news. It was suggested that we take the initiative and take some of Nicole's friends to visit her in hospital. Nicole told us who to bring and I very much wanted to be the member of staff to take them up to London. The parents of the four girls were very happy for this visit to take place. Nicola, Charlotte, Kerry and Rachel seemed very honoured to be asked because Nicole had many friends.

The Girls wanted to take as many items of support as they could from other members of Nicole's class and year group. Everybody was concerned for Nicole and wanted to wish her well, of course. But The Girls had never spoken to someone who was blind, and feared they wouldn't have anything to talk about. By taking cards and videos that she could hear The Girls would be able to describe to Nicole what sort of things her friends were up to and probably have a laugh about it.

There was no doubt that on the morning of the visit The Girls were excited but very nervous as to how the day might go. None of us could have predicted the outcome. The Girls were greeted at reception by Mrs Dryburgh whilst I went to park the minibus. By the time I reached the ward The Girls were beginning to talk but after Nicole had politely said hello to me, she told her mum to go away. We left quickly and let The Girls get on.

Mrs Dryburgh told me Nicole's diagnosis was beginning to become clear and it was suggesting everything we had feared. We talked and drank coffee for most of the day. As a parent myself it was like an emotional rollercoaster. We would go back occasionally to check they were all all right and discovered that they were talking very enthusiastically and having a great time. Nicole had saved her Christmas presents as Christmas had not taken place for the Dryburghs that year, so the bed was covered in the wrapping and content from many presents and cards that The Girls dutifully described to her. The hospital staff had provided a video and TV and Nicole was making sure that things went exactly the way she wanted. Eventually I dragged The Girls away; they were tired but so excited by the way the day had turned out.

Sometime after that day we had to arrange a meeting with the four girls and their mothers to discuss the issue of Nicole's diagnosis. Two community nurses advised me on whom to talk to about this. We sat in a small classroom and explained that Nicole would not survive this. It seemed to take a long time for the reality of what was being said to dawn on The Girls. As we explained the situation, it also began to sink in with me, and I too struggled to maintain my composure.

Luckily there were plenty of tissues to go around. The Girls' mothers were great and although I had to remain professional I wanted to hug them all – I wasn't sure whether it was for them or for me. I explained to The Girls that we would give them plenty of support to ensure they would see Nicole and do things with her. As soon as she came back from London a taxi was organised twice a week to take them to see her. I have nothing but admiration for those girls who have supported a friend through a time when things could not have been worse. In their early teens they had such a huge excuse not to work, with a distraction that very few teenagers would have to deal with. Yet they did no worse and mostly excelled in their SATs in Year 9 and GCSEs two years later.

I saw Nicole in my last few days at Barton Court before moving to Australia. Her determination to remain positive, active and happy has underlined her success in achieving so much. She has overcome so many of the psychological problems of blindness, she is determined to walk again and I understand is getting very close to it. She has written a book, learnt to ride, helped other people to deal with cancer and most of all coped with the thought that she was about to die herself.

I have learnt so much from knowing Nicole, whether it is how a young person can cope with such dire circumstances or what Justin Timberlake is really like. I find it hard to believe that I was ever paid to be her teacher.

The Girls

Rachel

Some things I remember clearly but others remain patchy and blurry. I remember the first time we went to visit Nicole in hospital in London. I felt scared, but happy at the same time as I would be seeing her. Another vivid day was the day we got told of the seriousness of Nicole's illness. I had been home from school that day and had taken a phone call from Mr Gugenheim (legend!) asking for my mum and me to come in to school the next day as there was to be a meeting about Nicole. He asked me not to tell the other girls, so as not to worry them. I was apprehensive all night as I felt it was going to be bad news.

Finally at lunch-time Mr Gugenheim came and collected the four of us and our mums from reception. We started talking about Nicole, how we felt and how she was. Then Mr G dropped the bombshell and told us that Nicole wasn't getting better. I started telling myself that it would be OK. Yes, she'd got cancer but things would carry on as normal for all of us. One of the mums asked how long she had got. At that moment, everything hit home. My eyes filled up and I looked around at the other girls – we were all filling up. We all cried. It didn't make it any better – there was no getting away from the reality of it. We spoke for a bit longer, don't even know what about, I am not sure if I was even listening, I was in sort of shock, frightened, sad, but most of all angry. How could this happen to someone so young and who had never done anything to deserve it? The adults went to the staffroom to chat, leaving us four girls to talk.

After I knew the seriousness of Nicole's illness I was very nervous and apprehensive about seeing her again. However, I was also determined not to get down about it when I was with her. We had to make the most of the time we had together.

But Nicole pulled through. I don't feel scared or nervous or apprehensive any more. I feel happy and really, really proud of her. Most weeks I open up the newspaper and find her in it, and she has been on the telly too. Nicole does loads for other people and never mopes about herself – she just gets on with life. She's a big inspiration to us all.

Kerry

When Nicole asked me to write about what has happened in the past few years, I started to worry. I was afraid to bring back all the memories at first. I had a barrier in my head stopping me writing down any of my feelings. In a way I didn't want to think back to how things had been. I tried putting it off for as long as I could.

One day that I remember as if it were yesterday, was when Charlotte, Nicola, Rachel, Mr Gugenheim and I went up to King's College Hospital to see Nicole for the first time since she'd collapsed in December 2002. We told everyone in our form and everyone was really supportive and gave us letters and cards. We collected money and bought Nicole a huge – and I mean huge! – Me To You Grey Bear.

We didn't stop singing all the way and couldn't wait to see Nicole. I remember the mood changing when we realised we were nearly there – we were listening to a tape and a slow song came on. I think it all suddenly hit us. I remember everyone getting emotional – I suppose we were all a bit scared. I hadn't really thought about it all in depth and I don't think any of us really knew what to expect. I remember we started holding hands on the way to Nicole's ward. We couldn't stop crying. But when we got to the ward something told us all to stop. We were there for Nicole and had to be strong.

Then it was just us five talking and gossiping like nothing had happened. To me nothing had changed, Nicole was still the same person.

Nicola

I can't remember clearly everything that happened to Nicole, but I can remember how I felt throughout the experience. It was difficult being fourteen years old, knowing one of your best friends was in hospital and not living the same kind of life as you any more. At times there were things you didn't think you could say because everything had changed for Nicole and it could have upset her.

These last three years, growing up with Nicole, have shown me how much her life has improved since she collapsed, and that's because of her determination to prove people wrong and do what they said she wouldn't be able to. I think she's amazing to turn her life around as she has done. And my life changed too, but you get used to it and the changes become normal. It was the little things that were different as well, like Nicole not being at school and not sending her silly letters in the post any more, but now at Christmas when Nicole opens a present, you just describe it to her without thinking about it. I'm lucky to have Nicole as a friend because she's made me a stronger person and I think she is amazing to get as far as she has, and she just keeps going!

Charlotte

I can still remember the day I found out that Nicole had been rushed to hospital; it was December and I was shopping in New Look in Canterbury, probably for Christmas presents. I was upstairs by the shoes and I remember my phone going off, it was a message from Nicola. I can't remember the exact words, but I know it was something along the lines of 'Nicole in coma, rushed to hospital in London after brain haemorrhage, can't speak, can't move'. I will never forget the feeling I had in my stomach when I read that text, it was so short and to the point, which was really unlike Nicola. I had to read it over and over for it to sink in and I think I was in New Look for about an hour just sitting there crying. It was and always will be the worst text I ever got.

The day we went to London. This was the day Kerry, Rachel, Nicola and I had been looking forward to and dreading at the same time. I can remember running to Safeway's before school to get flowers and grapes for Nicole, and we rushed back to the form room to collect everything; we had got Nic a huge grey bear, a big card from us all, and lots of letters to read to her. As we set off in the minibus with Mr Gugenheim (loveliest man ever!), all of us were really scared about what it was going to be like. We parked up outside what looked like the scariest, hugest hospital ever. We had to wait outside ages because we had bought Nicole one of those cards where you record your own message, and we didn't know what to say, and we kept getting it wrong! When we finally managed to record a decent message (I think Mr Gugenheim was pleased!) we went to meet Jackie and got the lift up to the floor Nicole was on. None of us could believe we were finally going to get to see Nicole again. I will never forget that lift journey; we were so nervous and scared and I held Kerry's hand really tightly because we were both crying and shaking. When we finally got to where Nicole was, I think we all just started crying; it was such a shock to see her looking so weak lying in bed.

We read letters, and gave her presents, and we just talked and talked for ages. Mr Gugenheim and Jackie kept putting their head around the corner asking if we were ready to go but Nicole said no! It was so good to be able to talk away normally face to face after everything that Nicole had been through. We talked about everything and Nicole told us all that she was allergic to the drug they were giving her, and how lucky she was to be alive. I couldn't believe how brave she was and it was really hard not to cry. Eventually though, reluctantly, we had to leave and say bye to Nic. The journey home was pretty silent; I think we were all exhausted and thinking about Nicole.

After everything that has happened and everything that Nicole has been through, I just can't believe how brave she has been. I don't know anyone else who could go through what she has and still come out on the other side with a determined smile on her face. The five of us girls have something really special and I am so glad that we have all had each other to stick by through the tough times. I can honestly say I am so proud and lucky to have the four best friends that I do and I hope it always stays that way. Nicole is the most amazing girl I know and I love her to pieces and always will.

Update

October 2007

A lot can happen in eight months. Especially in the world of me!

Three days after my 18th birthday I had my final round of chemo. I had a much lower dose because my heart and kidneys weren't strong enough to handle higher, but I was lucky to get that final round in. I finished my chemotherapy on the 15th February 2007. The 18th February would have marked three years in remission since my first lot of chemo, instead I was celebrating three days in remission.

On the morning of the 19th February I started to get an ache in my right hip and knee. By 2 p.m. my leg exploded with pain, and I was in absolute agony. I was screaming the house down! I knew almost immediately that it was another blood clot. Mum phoned for an ambulance but I wasn't allowed one because I was still breathing! I couldn't straighten or stand on my leg, but I eventually managed to get into my chair and in the car. Getting out of the car at the hospital, I twisted the ankle of my bad leg, so I was in agony by the time I got to the children's ward. I had an X-ray and an ultrasound which revealed a blood clot from above my hip to below my knee. No wonder it hurt! It was confusing because I was still on the daily anti-clotting injections to prevent another clot from forming. I had to stay in hospital for fifteen days: first of all for the clot, then because I kept getting infections in my Hickman line. The good news was that my hair started to grow back while I was in hospital. It was quicker than I had expected and it's curly again!

In March I had my first scan since my chemo ended, and that showed that my tumours had remained stable. I had my Hickman line taken out the next day as an emergency because it kept getting infected. I was glad it was gone, but it also meant it was back to having needles. I haven't had to stay in hospital since then, though, which I would have done if I still had my line. In a strange way I miss it, but I'm also so glad it's gone. I'm not paranoid now that I'll accidentally pull it out.

I finally got to go to CLIC Sargent's chocolate ball at the Dorchester Hotel in March. It was similar to the one I was too ill to go to in 2005, so I was chuffed to finally 'go to the ball'! That morning I found out that I was going to be offered a publishing deal. It was the news I had wanted to hear for three years, and it couldn't have come at a better time. I wasn't allowed to tell anyone until it was finalised, so I celebrated in secret that night.

I started back at college in March to continue with my English GCSE course, and tried really hard to catch up. I sat my exams in June. Both exams lasted over five and a half hours because I was allowed double time and rest breaks. I kept stopping for tea and cookie breaks too. I was in a room on my own with my support teacher and another teacher who read the questions to me. I took my laptop in to type my answers on. I found it OK, but remembered loads of things as soon as it finished that I should have written. I had really bad backache in the second exam so I couldn't wait to finish. I got my results at the end of August and I got a B grade. Annoyingly, though, I was just five marks below an A! But I was still pleased with a B. I decided not to go back to college. I'm going to see what happens in the next year.

I finally stopped having the anti-clotting injections in August. I had 246 in total. I can't believe I actually had that many. I still have to wear my sexy support stocking for another two years, but I'm so glad the injections have stopped. My needle phobia got really bad over the summer, but I've now found a solution . . . valium! I still have the phobia, but it just helps to calm me.

My fundraising for The Silver Lining Appeal has risen a lot since February, and I've now raised over £13,000. The neuro-rehabilitation room is going to be called 'Nicole's suite', which I'm over the moon about. The room will hopefully be used from summer 2008. If anyone reading this is unfortunate enough to have to use the room, I hope that it helps you recover.

From January I had been having trouble with my left ear. I was finding it a bit hard to hear, then I got a really bad pain and ringing in it. The hospital gave me paracetamol and put cotton wool in my ear to see if that helped, but it didn't, and my hearing got worse. I had a scan in August which showed I have an intracranial acoustic neuroma in each ear. They're small benign tumours. The damage in my left ear can't be repaired, and it sounds like I have less than 20% hearing left in that ear now. This is a sign of neurofibromatosis type 2. You may remember at the beginning of this book that I was suspected of having neurofibromatosis type 1. Well NF2 is much rarer! The diagnosis is still to be confirmed, but it's more than likely. From the end of November I'm going to have six weeks of daily radiotherapy to try and prevent any more damage to my hearing. It means travelling to The Royal Marsden Hospital again every day for five minutes of treatment. It feels like déjà vu seven years later!

We don't know what the future holds for me, but one thing's for sure, it'll be interesting! You can catch up with my news by visiting my website at www.c-h-o-c.org.uk

Goals

In 2005 I wrote a list of goals and people I wanted to meet. I had just met my favourite band Friday Hill which is something I'd always wanted to do. It made me write a list of other things I want to achieve. Here's the list. I've already managed to tick a few of them off!

I would like to meet . . .

- Blue
- Tara Palmer Tomkinson
- Elton John
- Ant 'n' Dec
- The Radio 1 DJs
- Dawn French and Lenny Henry
- Will Young
- Brian Dowling
- Kylie Minogue
- The Osbornes
- Lemar again (I don't want to stalk him though!)
- Richard and Judy

- Paul O'Grady
- Noel Gallagher
- Simon Cowell
- And the Queen (plus William and Harry)

I want to . . .

- Have hair down to my bra strap
- Be in an advert
- Be in *OK!* magazine
- Be a millionaire
- Wobble on the cobbles at Coronation Street
- Go sky-diving
- Do an abseil
- Walk in heels
- Go to New York
- Have my own documentary
- Publish this book which I have done because you're reading it

I wrote this poem when I was 16.

Rainbow

Nothing helps; stops the pain,
teardrops falling like acid rain.
Hearts are breaking, smiles are faking,
people pretending things are OK.
They don't live with it day after day.
Scared child in brave face –
nowhere to run, no air, no space –
It comes and goes, makes me a fighter
can ruin families but makes mine tighter.
It takes time to heal an open wound.
Sometimes it seems as if you're doomed.
Then you see a rainbow, shining bright.
That's what makes you decide to fight.
So whenever you're down or feeling blue,
remember that rainbow that pulled you through.

Glossary

Anaesthetic	A drug used to numb a part of the body (local anaesthetic), or to put a patient to sleep during surgery (general anaesthetic).
Anaesthetist	A doctor who specialises in giving patients anaesthetic.
Angiogram	An X-ray that creates images of blood vessels.
AVM	Stands for Arterio Venous Malformation. An abnormal collection of blood vessels.
Bells palsy	A condition which causes the patient to lose the function of one side of the face.
Benign	A term used to describe a non-cancerous tumour or a non-life threatening condition.
Biopsy	A test where a small sample of tissue is taken to be examined.
Blood clot	A clot of blood that forms inside the blood vessel.

Cannula	A tube that is inserted into a blood vessel, organ or duct, to inject fluid.
Catheter	A thin, hollow tube that is put into the bladder to drain urine.
Chemotherapy	A method to treat cancer by using a chemical substance that destroys cancerous cells.
CT scan	Stands for Computerised Tomography. A type of X-ray that uses a computer to create lots of cross-sectional images.
Dermatologist	A doctor that specialises in the treatment of skin.
DVT	Stands for Deep Vein Thrombosis which is when blood clots in a vessel, often the veins of the thighs or legs.
Echocardiogram	An ultrasound that uses sound waves to create an image of the heart's chambers and valves.
Haemorrhage	To bleed or lose blood extensively.
Hickman line	A long hollow tube made from silicone rubber that is inserted into a major vein. It can be used for taking blood tests and for giving chemotherapy.
Hydrotherapy	A form of physiotherapy carried out in water.

Ligament	They connect bones to each other and are made of fibrous tissue. They provide support while also allowing flexibility and movement.
Lumbar puncture	A procedure in which a hollow needle is inserted in the lower back in order to take a sample of fluid around the lower part of the spinal cord. This sample is then examined under a microscope.
Malignant	A term used to describe a cancerous tumour or a life-threatening condition.
Morphine	A drug that acts directly on the central nervous system to relieve pain.
MRI scan	Stands for Magnetic Resonance Imaging. A type of scan that takes detailed pictures by using magnets and radio waves.
Neurofibromatosis	A hereditary condition that mainly affects the nervous system and causes tumours to grow on nerves throughout the body. There are two types of the disease. NF1 is the most common type and NF2 is generally the more serious.
Neurosurgeon	A surgeon who specialises in operations on the brain and spinal cord.
Neutropenia	A fall in the number of white cells in the blood. White cells help protect from

infection, so people who have neutropenia have a greater risk of getting an infection. Chemotherapy may cause neutropenia.

Occupational therapist

Someone trained to help people manage their daily routine – e.g. dressing, cooking etc.

Oncologist

A doctor who specialises in the treatment of cancer.

Ophthalmologist

An eye doctor.

Optic nerve

The nerve that connects the eye to the brain.

Paediatrician

A doctor who specialises in treating children.

Paralysis

A term used to describe the loss of ability to use muscles.

Peripheral Nerve Sheath Tumour

Made up of tumours that develop from the nerves outside the brain or spinal cord (the peripheral nerves). Those who have inherited neurofibromatosis are at greater risk of developing PNST.

Phenytoin

A type of medicine often taken after brain surgery or a brain tumour to prevents fits.

Physiotherapist	A doctor who specialises in treatment that uses physical movements, massage and exercise to relieve illness or injury.
Radiographer	Someone who takes X-rays.
Radiotherapy	A treatment of cancer by using X-rays.
Scoliosis	A condition which causes the spine to curve to one side.
Spinal cord	A column of nervous tissue in the spinal column that sends messages between the brain and the rest of the body.
Steroids	Types of chemicals found naturally in the body, but are also produced artificially to treat diseases. Used to reduce the swelling surrounding brain tumours.
Stroke	A sudden attack of weakness affecting one side of the body.
Tumour	Any abnormal swelling on the body can be called a tumour. They can be either benign or malignant.
Ultrasound	A way of producing pictures of the inside of the body using sound waves.
Whiplash	When muscles, ligaments and tendons in the neck stretch and strain, often caused by sudden jerks or jolts to the body.

Charities

And now to thank the charities. Without these, I wouldn't have been able to do, go to or get through some of the things I have. They've all been a part of my recovery in various ways, and for that I thank them all.

CLIC Sargent is the UK's leading children's cancer charity. They give support to children and young people diagnosed with cancer. They used to be two charities, CLIC (Cancer and Leukemia in Children) and Sargent Cancer Care for Children. They joined together in 2005. They offer a range of services from clinical care through CLIC Sargent nurses and doctors, short holidays to Malcolm Sargent House in Scotland or to one of their caravans, free accommodation near to the hospital where a child is having treatment, research into childhood cancers, and emotional and financial support for the child and their families. My CLIC Sargent nurses have been brilliant and have had to tell me some difficult things over the years. They are always on the end of the phone if Mum ever needs them, or just wants some advice, and they come to the house if I'm not feeling well. Best of all, the colour of CLIC Sargent's logo is fuschia!

Website: www.clicsargent.org.uk

Demelza House is an eight-bed house built in six acres of countryside in Bobbington near Sittingbourne, Kent. It was built in 1998 in memory of Demelza James who died of a brain tumour in 1990 at the age of 24. She worked at a children's hospice in Birmingham, and loved her job. Her parents realised that the South East didn't have anything like this, so they decided to fund-raise to build a hospice near where they live. Demelza House offers residential hospice care to over 450 children and young adults from Kent, East Sussex and South London with life-limiting illnesses, who aren't expected to reach adulthood. They provide respite, symptom control, end of life care and bereavement support. They need £3.5 million a year to keep running, and they rely almost completely on donations. I love going to Demelza, and it feels like my second home now. The only bad side to it is that you have to prepare yourself for 'the phonecall'. I dread phonecalls from Demelza in case it's to tell me one of my friends has died. I've had two of those calls, but there is a lovely area in the garden where friends and family can plant things or leave ornaments in memory of their loved one. It's called the fairy garden. Demelza House became Demelza in 2006, as there is now a 'Demelza James home from home' service in East Sussex, and a 'Demelza Child' in East London. Demelza's slogan is 'Adding life to days, when days cannot be added to life'. This is exactly what they do.

Website: www.demelzahouse.org

I'm an ambassador for the **Silver Lining Appeal** at King's College Hospital in London. King's embarked on an £8 million project in 2004 to create a modern, state of the art environment, which includes a new children's ward, a new children's critical care centre and an enlarged liver unit. King's College Hospital is nationally renowned for their excellent work in specialist fields. They provide the largest children's liver service in the world, and they are a specialist children's centre for Cystic Fibrosis, diabetes, asthma and brain surgery. The Silver Lining Appeal was created to run alongside the refurbishment to raise £400,000 to purchase new medical equipment for the wards. I wanted to help them in a big way because it's a fantastic hospital, so I contacted them to see how I could help. They said they needed £30,000 to buy specialist equipment for a neuro-rehabilitation room. It was exactly the kind of thing I wanted to fund-raise for. I

could have done with a room like that while I was staying at King's, which is why I'm determined to raise the money needed so that children in the future have a better chance of recovery after brain and spinal injuries.
Website: www.kch.nhs.uk/fundraising/support/sl

I am also an ambassador for **MOVE**, which stands for **Mobility Opportunities Via Education**. It is a physio programme for severely disabled children which I joined in January 2006 as one of the first adolescents on the scheme. MOVE teaches basic movement skills that most of us take for granted, such as sitting, standing and walking, to severely disabled children to help them with independence. Each child has their own programme to suit their needs and goals. They reach little targets along the way. My goal was to walk with Mum on one side and a stick on the other by December 2006. I wasn't able to achieve that due to my relapse, but it's still my goal for the future. I've got so much stronger since being on the MOVE programme, and I owe a lot to my dedicated physiotherapists, Kamala and Julie. MOVE's aim is to give all 110,000 severely disabled children in the UK access to the programme – because everyone deserves the chance to MOVE.
Website: www.move-europe.org.uk

The Riding for the Disabled Association (RDA) was founded in 1969. They help people with disabilities improve health and gain confidence through riding and carriage driving. Riding can improve several things, including balance, posture and muscle tone. Those that are unable to ride drive the carriages. RDA has over 500 groups, which help over 25,000 children and adults a year. There are special competitions and tests that RDA riders can do. I've done a few of them. I love riding, and it has definitely improved my strength. One of the first things someone said to me when I started riding was, 'The best thing for the inside of a woman, is the outside of a horse!' It's one of those quotes I'll never forget.
Website: www.riding-for-disabled.org.uk

I joined **Post Pals** in 2006. It's a website for poorly children, and the aim is to 'post a smile on a sick child's face'. Each 'Pal' has their own page with their details, things they like, updates and a forwarding address. Anyone can write to them or send them a gift to cheer them up when they're ill. Post Pals was set up in 2004 by five teenagers who all have health problems, with two of them being bed bound. They're all volunteers, and spend a lot of time sending post to the 'Pals'. I've received letters, cards and presents from all over the world. I got a lot of post when I relapsed. I made a comment on my website that I wanted to get a pink wig, and someone sent me seven in different styles and shades of pink – one for each day of the week – and a pink cowboy hat. It really did make me smile. I was also sent 'chemo duck', who is the coolest duck ever. He has little pyjamas on, and when you open his top he has a plaster on under it. When you take that off, he has a little plastic Hickman line in his chest. He's to help children get through their treatment. He also has a bandana because he's lost his feathers, bless him. Another one of my favourite things is that someone adopted a monkey for me in North Carolina. That's something I've wanted to do for as long as I can remember, as monkeys are my favourite animal. Post Pals is a fantastic site, and does a great job. If you have a spare five minutes, write to a child and help make them smile!

Website: www.postpals.co.uk

Dave Lee's Happy Holidays is a charity that was set up in 1994 by comedian and local legend, Dave Lee. The charity sends underprivileged, sick and disabled children in Kent on holiday or for a special day out with their immediate family. Dave Lee has been in the entertainment business for over 25 years, and is best known for being one of the country's top stand-up comedians. No one involved in the charity is paid. To date, Dave Lee's Happy Holidays have given nearly 20,000 children in Kent a holiday or special day out. When I was really poorly they paid for my two limo trips to Bluewater with my friends. It made my shopping trip more special, and much more comfy!

Website: www.daveleeshappyholidays.org.uk

The **Kent Association for the Blind (KAB)** was set up in 1920 to help blind and partially sighted people in Kent. They offer counselling, information and advice on being blind, encourage people to increase their independence and safety, provide equipment to help with everyday activities, and they also record and distribute talking newspapers and magazines. I had help from the KAB for a year from Steve Mitchell. He gave me home lessons on how to use my talking laptop. He also taught me how to send emails and use the Internet, and I haven't looked back since.

Website: www.kab.org.uk

The **Talking Newspapers Association of the United Kingdom (TNAUK)** was set up in 1974, providing national newspapers and magazines for visually impaired and disabled people. They read over 250 newspapers and magazines on to various formats, including CDs and cassettes. They're sent through the post in little wallets with reversible address labels in a pocket on the front. One side has my address, and the other has TNAUK's. It's easy to just reverse the label and post them back. I get a few magazines which means I'm always up to date with news and gossip.

Website: www.tnauk.org.uk

Acknowledgements

I accept no responsibility for your emotional state by the time you reach this page. Especially you, Julie!

There are so many people I have to thank, so if you're not mentioned here please don't think I've forgotten you. You're in my thoughts.

To all the doctors and nurses that have cared for me over the last seven years, especially Dr Martin, Dr McCormick and Darren Hargraves. Thank you for always being honest with me. Thank you too to the Children's Community Nurses. The biggest thanks, though, has to go to the charming and talented Chris Chandler. Without you I wouldn't be here, and for that you're my hero. A true legend. Thank you.

To all my family and friends. Hilary and John (thanks for all the fudge and chocolate over the years), Sue (old lady – the zimmer's still in the post!). My amazing best friends, Nicola, Rachel, Charlotte and Kerry. You stuck by me when it really mattered, and I'll never forget that. Love you all for ever.

To everyone at *City Hospital*. Thanks for the support.

To Nadia and Andi for making it fun, Gemma for finding me in the first place and Nick for always making me laugh. I knew you'd moan, Nick, if you didn't get a thank you! You know I love you really.

To Simon who is always willing to drive us to London. Love the gossip, Simondo!

A big mwah! to Gilly and Frances for making my eyebrows perfect and doing my make-up for the front cover.

Thank you to everyone who helped get my book off the ground. To all at the *TES*: Sarah, Geraldine, Jill. A big thank you to my agent Lindsey Fraser and to all at Hodder: Margaret, Naomi, Nicola and David. Thank you for being the ones to give me the chance, and for believing in me.

A massive thank you to Evelyn. Without your hard work this book wouldn't have been possible. I know it's taken a long time and I have frustrated the hell out of you with my stubbornness, but hopefully it's all been worth it, and we got there in the end! Plus you have to admit our 'book meetings' were fun, and we ate a lot of cake! Thank you too for all the other help you give us, and to Alexander for the technical help with my laptop.

Finally but most importantly Mum, Lee, Molly and Daizy. You're what keep me going and keep me laughing. Leeroy, I know we don't do the lovey-dovey brother/sister thing, but I think you rock and I love you. Molly and Daizy, I know you can't read this, but I had to give you a mention. You're the most important things to me, and you keep me smiling. And Mum, I stand by what it says on the fridge magnet I got you years ago . . . *If mums were flowers, I'd pick you!* I know I'm a bit of a handful, but thank you for putting up with me and my diva demands!

Love you all xxx

Idiot.